RED
AND
WHITE
STARLIGHT
SKY

MATT P.J. SCHELLENBERG

Red and White Starlight Sky
Copyright © 2023 by Matt P.J. Schellenberg

Tellwell Talent
www.tellwell.ca

ISBN
978-0-2288-9548-0 (Paperback)
978-0-2288-9549-7 (eBook)

For my friend, Shelly de Waal

Table of Contents

Not the Noise

It's not the noise that bothers me,
It's the silence my heart makes
When she's not around.

I Bought This Stupid Shirt Just to Flirt with You

You rubbed off on my heart too easily,
And now I keep thinking of you
Without knowing your name.

Will divinity bring us back
To that holy moment?

Could it ever?

'Cause I was paralyzed
Next to you, couldn't even
Look away when all the emerald
In the world is nothing
Compared to your eyes.

Funny you have to almost meet your end
To finally live. I have thanked my angels
For this; they kept me alive long enough
To lead me to you….

Jonesin'

Save me from this treachery darlin'.
When I look at you, I see
Everything I've ever wanted
Sparkling bright in your eyes.
You're straight blue fire,
You're Saturn minus the rings.
And I'm not one to fall in love,
But I think I'm jonesin' right now.
When I look at you, I see
Life in a dead world.
You're screaming attraction
Without using your voice.
And now it's all I can hear.

Every Time I Breathe

You keep my days full of light
And my heart silently
Beating for a dream
Underneath the stars.
Never wanting to move
On from this moment
Tiptoeing away in silence.
Never wanting to let go.
Oh, I could leave all these
Questions in the wake of my glow,
But it wouldn't be the same.
It wouldn't be enough to never know why
You are so hypnotic,
And I still fall madly for it every time.
Every time I breathe,
I breathe in for you and exhale for me.

Secret Admirer

I wanna tell you I've been holding
Something in for years.
But I'm afraid that if I tell you, you'll never
Talk to me again.
Despite how often I've seen you lately,
I'm afraid it would be never
As opposed to months.
I want you to be happy regardless
Of your thoughts about me,
If there are any thoughts.
I've been intoxicated by you since our first encounter.
I thought meeting you was dreamy,
Thought it was surreal.
And even though I may mean
Nothing to you,
You have always been
A planet I've wanted to travel to.
I just know that if I ever got there
I'd never wanna leave.

Dopamine

You're the reoccurring file,
The one that pops up time
And time again without fail.
Despite the daggers in me
I'm still burning crazy
Beautiful love lines in notebooks,
Collecting dust on the shelves.
I didn't use to live like this,
Surviving off dopamine surges
From every single word
I get you to say.

The Beauty of Our Situation

We're distant,
But we could be close fast.
'Cause I can be on Broadway
In under twenty minutes.
I will let you taste
What I already know
About flavour.
Thank God we met before final rest.
The beauty of our situation being
That this red diamond is nothing compared
To even the shadow of you.

As She Rides

The colours reflected in her eyes, flawless and hypnotic.
Her smile saved my life from deep blue suicide.
I've been trying to find purpose,
And I found it in her device;
Soon as she walked through the door,
I became enlightened by the sound of her gorgeous voice
As she rode her war horse into the battle of midnight.

I.O.U.

It only takes a smile from you
To make me feel like I've aced life,
Like I won the lottery, like I've inherited
An endless supply of blessings,
Like I'm surfing on Saturn's rings.
I owe you so much more than I can give
For my happiness.

I Hope Tonight

I hope tonight will lull you to sleep
And in dreams maybe we'll meet
Feeding our selfish desires
And starting fires from the friction
Provided between us.
Whadda you think, interested in a ring?
We could hop on a plane
And spin around and around.
We'll take pictures and share the bed,
We'll kiss and dream out loud.
I'm daydreaming of your lips
And how it would complete me
To work your hips and whisper
"I love all your tricks, words,
Passions and nerves."
And how I wish—
Oh, how I wish—
You'd love me till
I'm part of a cemetery.

Make It up to You

I was such a fool to
Walk out on you that night.
I was unstable like a kettle boiling;
I went off, chemically unbalanced.

Could I ever make
It up to you enough
In five hundred
Billion lifetimes?

My main objective
Would always be
To make it home to you
Alive and in one piece
Every single moment
Until my lights went out.

Rarity

To them you're only eye candy,
But to me you're a rarity.
Like a red rose always in bloom,
Even in winter, or an angel touring Earth,
With work to do.
Maybe I should make a move to
You, soon.
Or maybe I should ride my war horse
All the way back home.

Oh, Beautiful Deep Blue

\Oh, beautiful deep blue of her eyes,
Many have drifted and become lost in them.
Her ocean floor is covered in skeletons
And sunken ships,
And I'm trying not to join the dead just yet.
I cling to the wheel,
As your storm approaches.

The Cougar

Judging by your beauty,
I can tell you're used to
Men falling to their knees
To worship you
Every second of the day.
Calling you stunning,
Calling you gorgeous,
Calling you sexy.
And they're right of course,
But I believe you are more.
I could find you a perfect ring
If you'd stick around to know me,.
If you'd listen to this hopeless
Romantic heart promise
Unquestionable love and loyalty
To the grave.

Eyes up Here

I once knew an unstoppable force
Who navigated effortlessly around
Every single obstacle.

She did it all so fast,
I'm sure that heart of hers almost burst out
Screaming during the car crash
Of last night
In the dying seconds of 11:59 P.M.

Thought mine would leave me
The same way.

The first time I saw her,
My eyes dilated
As I struggled
To comprehend and process
How beautiful
The image was before me.

What a magnificent creature,
How can it get anymore
Gorgeous than her?

She was standing in line
Getting groceries,
Fully aware that her presence
Was dropping the jaws of every
Single person around her.

Someone like that demands
Attention, gets more than she needs to
Always keep her tires full.

And I could tell,
It made her smile
Even louder.

The Golden Queen

She teaches dance,
What a golden queen.
I could write an anthology about her
If she knew I was alive,
If she read my works,
If she winked or smiled.
We could be like two fierce
Tigers in a cartoon city.

A Halo and a Pair of Wings

Her smile was a halo and a pair of wings,
Attracting angels and beautiful things to her light,
Before she said, "Goodbye, handsome.
Oh, goodbye forever with my last breath and kiss.
Will you miss my dialogue when I'm no longer
Here to write you poems and songs in the mist?"

Off Come Our Boots

Her smile alone
Could grant all of Earth starlight.

Her laugh
Melts icebergs
From this scarred heart,
Shakes the demons
Off shoulder blades.

Her voice alone
Gives me dragon wings.

Oh, I think I might try now,
Time to practice a different
Kind of art form.

'Cause by the way things
Are forming, I'm gonna be moving
Backward just as fast as forward.

Off come our boots...

Heavy

As it is, I'm not vacant upstairs
Or missing a pulse.
I choose to keep this fire
Inside my chest, hoping for the best
And the rest will follow.
She tried to blow out all my candles,
But stopped when I kissed her
Goodnight under a full moon,
Our tongues dancing to a slow beat.
It was heavy, until I woke up.

And Tonight She Will

The paint brushes
Are inside her head.

She uses them
When she speaks,
When she moves.

And when she smiles
Legions go weak
In the knees and fall to them.

In a heart beat
She could shake a nation
With the colours
Of her language.

And tonight she will.

With These Brushes Dipped in Dreams

Close your eyes,
Let the music take over and fill you up.
Find a brush and paint; colours will cooperate.
Find a brush and paint because one day,
Your tickets will be no good.
In this painter's den
With these brushes dipped in dreams
I'll spill over canvas, unleashing what I carry inside
That language cannot describe.

Daydream Me

As you move to that place I can't go,
Remember yesterday, daydream me while you
Sing heavenly songs to God, say hello.
One day we'll be in the same spot.
Are you only here for the year?
For the ride?
You reside in my mind since we locked eyes.
Who decides if it's true love or a cruel sign?
Daydream me if you can.

Some Night in 2010

I was spray painting a tiger on wheels,
Driving a wooden car through a library last night.
In my dream, it all made sense.

The Last Thing She Said to Me

My dream last night took
Me for a ride;
We walked on the beach
And swam in the lake where
You said "Never forget this
Moment, okay, hun?
Never forget this kiss goodbye,
Until we reconnect again in the sky city."

Hoping to Illuminate

I play this song for hours,
For days, and it's like
Swimming in hot springs
At home in my own space,
Still amazed,
Dreaming of her
To pave the way
To recovery.
I'm sorry, but
Why can't I play
The hero tonight?
I'm always a grey shadow dream,
Hoping to illuminate.

In Last Night's Travels

In last night's travels, in last night's dream,
I could feel the tropical breeze,
And see and hear jungle animals,
Calm, chef's kiss perfect picture moments,
But you're telling me it's not real?
You were in your element—
Soon I'll be walking in mine—
Of frozen temperatures and ice.
I continue to cling to your promise,
Of living forever with my maker.

That's the Dream

I hold onto this dream so tightly,
I'm worried it won't be able to breathe.

The Door of My Discovery

Inside of the realms of sleep,
I was aware, trying to write poetry.
I forgot those surreal lines except one,
And what I did find was a mystery,
A note written down for me to read.
Saying, "This is the door of my discovery."
Is it somewhere ahead of me, waiting for
Me to step through, and see?

Dragon Slayer

On the wall, a bleeding heart,
Right next to a skull surrounded by ruby roses.
My version of a dream catcher.
I rose this morning ripped from my dreams,
But I wish I was still there.
I was a knight, fighting a dragon in his lair.
I went down more than once, but I kept pushing forward
Till I held its severed head in my hands.
I was a hero on my way to collect my reward,
When I woke up to jazz music
And the smell of coffee, bacon and eggs.
She said, "Where were you just now?"
I was leaping through time looking for you.

I Leave My Dreams in the Ink

He whispered to her gravestone,
"Your heart was a wave, in a sea of sorrows.
I used to get sick and shipwrecked all the time,
So easily swallowed,
Propelled from the boat to the rocks of you,
The island of you, where you won't let me die alone.
You bring life and purpose to this weathering suit.
You check up on me every blue moon and fortnight
To see if I'm still smoking or if I've kicked the habit.
I've only grown more obsessed
With filling up blank pages with my soul's signature.
I leave my dreams in the ink..."

Legion

My words are legion,
They are my army
When the enemy
Thinks I'm outnumbered.
I can stop a band of fiends
In their tracks with a few sentences,
I just can't stop myself...

Awake, I Write to Thee

Awake, I write to thee.
Safe haven found only when I sleep,
Lay my head down off to dream.
Should I kill these projections or make peace?
I have extracted words before.
I woke up, wrote them down.
Then off again to that far place I went.
Off to save the world.
Off to fend off the wolves from my den.

Oh, So That's What You Ink?

If I can capture lightning from
The storm of tonight,
I'll be satisfied.
I'm grateful I can be random,
Letting my heart take
Me on adventures.
I'll go to that coffee shop
And focus on my manuscripts.
They constantly whisper my name in the wind.

Master of Works You've Never Heard of

I am a Master of Works you've never heard of,
So read them now I say.
And I am a natural disaster coming down this way.
I will rip away sentimental moments only to play
A song that never gets old, and sing a melody
That never goes off key.

Don't Retire the Pen

It's been years since I've wandered
Those streets; the haunted path still beckons me.
I have no plans on returning, for the
Fire that's burning within whispers,
"Move on, warrior, don't backtrack.
You are a blue planet that once was
Home to aftermath.
You are a priceless jewel, still shining,
Heavenly bright with red and white starlight
Inside your mind; don't follow the pack,
And don't retire the pen until you're bones."

Standing Tall

I daydream too much, starry-eyed, wide awake and hopeless.
I often see angels in every direction;
They blend in with every golden heart.
But I just wanna be remembered
For having starlight in my mind's eye.
I must continue this obsession;
If I don't do this, I will die unfulfilled.
It's in my blood, always has been.
Even as a boy, I knew that no matter how fast or far I went
That I would never ghost it.
So I stand tall now, ready to act the role
That was always mine,
Flowing from the ink left behind my war path.

That's Your Superpower? Lame.

You move, with a purpose,
So determined to find a glimpse of heaven.
"I wonder when I'll see the real thing,"
He said to himself.
Well, only in degrees, here and there,
A hummingbird moth visiting the yard in July,
A blue jay singing songs by the pond
Up the stairs and to the right.
A blonde to die for, smiling back at me
Before leaving my life.
It won't matter
When you're bones.
If I could only stop pain
With a pen...

But the Writing

You were practically my pulse,
And dancing on the spot alone,
All I can do is two step with your ghost.
I can't sing a note like you did;
My voice refuses to leave my throat.
So, I'll spell it out instead.
You were my paradise,
My endless river of life.
And now it's almost run dry.
I said, "But the writing…"
As I forced back tears.
The writing keeps fear distant
And me from breaking down
The walls of my own dam.
The dam must hold because
You were once a universe of healing,
And now I drift off into the atmosphere
Hoping to catch the attention
Of your red and white starlight sky.

Your Prayers Are Pink Diamonds

Deep in the forests of my mind, deep in a dream,
I met an old friend who told me that every prayer
Becomes a pink diamond in your hands.
We both said the warmest of intentions we had,
Words of love and hope, and then she faded
Into the background as the scene changed,
And I sat next to a fire pit,
Singing a song I had never heard before,
Until I woke up, whispering,
"Your prayers are pink diamonds."

Jewel

Escape the city, join the river,
Flow, it's always busy.
Listen to the roar of nature's voice out here.
No one holding you back, no one talking trash,
No one cutting you down, just the current
Flowing free all around.
Join me up north, baby,
Sleeping bags, fire pit, endless stars.
I'll never be over this jewel of a moon shining now,
Lighting up the ground and everything around me,
Calming my soul.
Oh, you know I've waited so long to regain control.
I've waited so long to sing this song, jewel of my life.

The Battle Inside Your Head

I got stuck on Broadway today;
It stormed hissing snakes
And howling wolves for hours.
I stayed catching up with someone
In the grip of a mental illness.
The battle inside your head
Rages on, but I know what it's like when
The mind screams "Die! Go on take your life!"
And I pray you recover from
This test of the will 'cause
It's a battle for your soul,
But no one says a word,
Like it might hurt.
Look to the clouds,
And remember
You could be a citizen of Heaven if you
Stay loyal to the light.

Watch Over Me

Be with me as I wait,
Watching the clock's hands tick, and tock.
Watch over me and be my lantern in the cold dark night.
For the world out there is full of hungry beasts,
And I may not survive the night without your angels.
I may not survive myself...

Mad as I Used to Be

Maybe I haven't been honest about what it is I want,
'Cause I can't be present when I'm already gone.
I haven't told you why I'm waiting
In this coffee shop alone.
Think the truth would make you hate your phone.
Think the truth would drive you mad,
Mad as I ever was,
Mad as I used to be.

Grenade

Sifting through old material,
I totally forgot about these
Scattered recollections
Of a blurry nightmare.

The doc said,
"Take your meds,
And take your meds
And take your meds."

It was terrifying losing it all again,
The blur of madness,
Where my reality was spent
With a polluted mind, darkness
Was legion.

And I remember thinking,
"Tonight was a miracle,
And a close call...
It was just like you said:
I almost pulled the pin."

Grandpa's Ring

I used to wear a silver ring, for Grandpa.
But I stopped.
I'm sorry I lost the gold one.
This is for newfound friendship
And the return of poetry in my life.
Still, I know it was always there.

Without a Tombstone

I can't get ahead
While I'm being
Weighed down
By the sins of a grandfather
I've never met.
And while I would love
To be able to forgive him someday,
Right now, deep down, I hope he's been buried
Without a tombstone, swallowed up
By the earth's vengeance.

Hospital Conversation

I won't be able to
Tell you my story
If I'm too busy
Pacing back and forth
In the waiting room.

You said, "What now?"
As the sickness continued to drain your
Life force in a hospital bed.

I held your hand,
As you drew closer
To the next realm.

Your firefly light was
Starting to dim, I could tell.

You stared at me,
With tears in your eyes
And I told you I loved you.

You whispered,
"I know, I'm on my way out,
Ask me what's
On your mind

Before I go."

Will you guide me,
When you become a spirit?

"Of course,
Did you even need to ask?"

A Letter Meant for You (Part 2)

I used to be an extra limb,
A cold extension of you,
But gone are the days of recognition,
Replaced with years of me becoming
A stranger when we were blood all along.
I can't get that time back and I still
Struggle with the death of yesterday.
I wish I knew you better,
I wish we could be civil.
I do love you,
Despite distance and everything
Said by silence.

Searching High and Low

He started climbing the tallest mountain
He could find, thinking he would be able
To speak with his maker.
But as he made his ascent, he heard a voice inside whisper,
"You've been looking for me, but I've been right here
This entire time waiting for this moment.
I've always been a sentinel,
And holy light that loves you beyond comprehension.
If you would only open your heart,
I would make you whole while you're searching high and low.
I'm right here, daydreamer.
Dream of me, and I will show you my world."

Lifeline

A cool northern breeze passes.
Birds in flight land on fences to sing their
Love songs, so I listen like my life depends
On memorizing their melodies.
My heart beats slow and
Steady like a sloth moving through a tree.
I drift off to the mountains where
My brother defeats them,
Where he is happiest,
And my sister and brother-in-law sit
On the beach, watching the ocean waves.
I smile for the first time, feeling like I'm not haunted
By words I never got to say.
My mind dances on the spot because
The sun is brilliant and shining
And summer is right around the corner.
I'm anxious for its promise of thunderstorms.
You are my lifeline, when my life is at war.

Either Way

You still play in the city,
Down by the snow-covered trail.
You play heartache songs
That make people fall to the floor in tears.
Here, wipe your eyes with this and listen;
Every mistake is a battle scar on your beautiful soul.
Every ounce of emotion would be left to rot,
If I didn't do this every day,
Capturing time in a poem,
And right now, there are books collecting dust.
I will find you all homes.
Dear books, I will find
You a spot in the shelves, row by row.
Told you I would do this;
I told you this before:
I would leave this place for dead
In a second if I could, 'cause
I need ocean air,
While I drink medium roast coffee,
And eat blackberries.
I need the mountains;
That's where my blood lives.
Wherever there are mountains,
Brother, you are there.

I can see it now,
In love with the mountains
Until you retire, and even after
Still, you'll love it some more.
Wherever there is an ocean,
Sister, you'll be there
Letting Tambo unleash his inner wolf.
I know you two will accomplish
Whatever you put your minds to.
You've always been robins and blue jays
Singing on the fences of my life.
Your kindness is ineffable, like a beautiful dream.
And like a dream,
I fail to capture its details.
And then one day you're turning thirty-eight,
And you know you still haven't really lived.
And that wilderness
In you wants out
Of its room to play like
Last night's dream where
A woman smiled and whispered,
"You ache for someone
Crashing into your life,
So you can fall hard for her.
Sapphire eyes feed on smiles,
Or maybe it's lust,
But either way, you win tonight."

Had I Not Been Where I Was

There will always be a connection to this place;
This was where I stopped by, broken and freezing.
That memory lingers like the aftermath of a tornado.
I thought my world was ending,
That my chapters were already written,
And that I was watching the credits rolling.
Had I not been where I was,
You wouldn't be reading this book.

Friends and Fam

When I am no longer here for
Talks and walks of life,
Friends and Fam, please know
If I go before you, that I'll be your guiding angel.
You got me through battles
Against F5 tornados,
Off-the-charts earthquakes,
Erupting volcanos,
Raging forest fires,
Unexpected floods and a condition
I keep under control with pills and needles,
But you were my medicine
Before I needed any.

Poems in the Sand

I woke up, falling like a comet,
Until I hit the water.
I swam to the shore
In search of aid,
And found none.
I am alone with skeletons,
Missing limbs,
Clutching weapons.
Last thing I remember
Was being on the train,
Having a wonderful dinner and not thinking
About my problems back home.
She was enchanting,
And to die for, Mandy, she said her name was Mandy,
Who absolutely loved pandas to the point of obsession.
We drank tequila shots and red wine,
And talked about our passions.
I guess it doesn't matter now,
Nothing could've prepared me for
This land of the forgotten,
Where I will spend my days writing
Poems In the sand unless I'm rescued.

Hourglass

Annihilate fear,
Stress, worry and doubt.
Give it to Him, that's not what you're all about,
That's not how He made you.
Dear soul, rise anew
As you welcome
Today's hourglass.
Remember that no matter how hard
You try to grasp it, it will pass through
Your hands and leave you in reflection,
Desperately trying to remember
How the moment used to feel.

One Big Alarm Clock

So many people snooze through life,
In a haze, in a blur, trying to kill bad memories.
They need someone to hit one big alarm clock.
Hit it for them and show them the way.
But we don't know the way, no
Some of us have no direction but down.
And it won't change until you take your own steps,
And carve something out of nothing with your own hands.
One big alarm clock, and so many dying to hear the sound.

Who Has the Time?

I hear His voice through
Yours, and it's calming.
"Enjoy it while you can," she said,
"'Cause the end is coming
Like an asteroid en route to Earth."
Lately it feels like we're
Living in the moments before a supernova.
So, breathe long and hard while
You're walking on solid ground,
'Cause we're destined to be left behind soon
And forgotten but welcomed above.
Just know when my eyes close for good,
I'll be travelling through
The spiritual realm.
Take His hand and witness
A glimpse of what rewards await
Those who believe and knock upon on His door.
But who has the time for salvation anymore?

Caffeine is My Life Blood

After the alarm clock goes off,
I slide out of bed and make my way
To the coffee pot, putting in three heaping cups
Of ground medium roast,
Add water and wait for it to kick in and save my life again.
My very close friend, I always give in to taste
Your rich flavour and inhale your bold aroma as I finish my
First poem of the morning.
You keep me from dozing back to sleep
Following a wild grinning cat.
I can still walk in the spirit world
While I'm awake;
I've done it before.

Have You Noticed My Absence?

I came into your store almost everyday to
Work on my dreams.
Have you noticed the space by the windows where
My thousand-mile stare reigned like a shockwave?
I'd often daydream of you walking beside me,
Deep in your ways, lost in thoughts of beautiful ideas.
Wherever you rest your head now, I won't forget
The way you had mine spinning from the first time seeing
You alive and thriving.
I hope it's not the last time you land near me, angel.

Over Lunch

I stepped out for a minute,
Where my taste buds enjoyed
The heart-to-heart conversation
Over lunch and coffee.
Next time it's on me.
So far, I'm loving this five-minute walk
Down the street,
Where I can focus on my dream
One poem at a time.
Right now, I wanna know where I
Stand, if I'm standing at all...

Hobbies

I'm alive, up and running
After two cups of coffee.
Your smile nukes my depression
And burdens off my shoulders.
I could go on, so I will:
You fix broken hearts like it's a hobby.
You fixed me, without even trying.

Coffee and Conversation

It's the women
Still up at 2:30
In the morning
That I want to talk to.

It's the souls
Who are screaming
Inside because they're alone.

Maybe we could fix that with coffee

And conversation.

At the Table

It was pouring outside.
He sat by the windowpane and stared
At the city below, at the tiny dots,
The lights left on so far away and calm.
He could almost hear her voice through
The glass, and the noise of the club reminded him
At last, to be present.
Lately he'd been going solo sitting at the table
On the far right, watching the candles flicker.
He ordered a coffee so he could stay up all night
Remembering her as only he could.
Her wilderness haunted him still, like she'd never left.

Closing Time

Inside, the coffee shop is closed.
She's ringing in the totals
For the day, remembering
The customers and
The words that stayed
Long after they had made leave.
She whispered to herself,
"It's always better when
You're here to ward off the darkness
With a lantern in the night.
I didn't say a thing,
When I could've decimated
Your heart in seconds.
I chose to be a vault of silence;
The combination
Changes whenever I'm bored."

Carnage

Darkness pours out into
The evening. I unravel layers and
Bare my soul to two lovely maidens,
The keepers of caffeine.
My thoughts flood my skull like pedestrians
On a Japanese crosswalk.
Beautiful clarity, I swim in the aftermath of spent years.
I come up for air and exhale my burdens in crisp September.
Oh, time, oh past loves, you never saw my path,
Never knew my potential, but neither did I until
It made its way into my life.
I am devoted to the pen like a possessed
Man eating lion, leaving carnage.

I Dreamt I Was King

I dreamt I was king,
Made of pale skin.
So was my queen.
We created a blizzard of words,
Watched the snow fall,
Carefully treading on black ice,
Saying maybe we're more
Than January frost.
Maybe we're supernatural
Siberian tigers on the prowl for jugulars.

They're Alive

In my cave, I blow out smoke,
Restless as a coiled cobra,
Sleepless as an insomnia-ridden bear
With months of cold to kill.
I've got boxes of books without homes
Just sitting in my doorway.
I've got a desire to keep
Doing the work;
The rest will come soon enough.
I remember you saying "Patience,
You're up next, knock 'em dead, stunner."
This is what sustains me,
Keeps me interested in living.
My poems are Koi fish carelessly swimming in ponds.
They are blood drunk tigers,
Swarming giant hornets,
Furious fire ants,
Deadly man of war jellyfish,
Ghostly stingrays
And terrifying great white sharks.
They're alive, and they capture me in time.

Chrysalis

Beneath your chrysalis, you stir;
Your design is shifting.
A great metamorphosis
Will soon take place
Beneath the stars.
You will one day emerge
And become one yourself.
As you spread your wings and take flight,
You will soar above this realm
And become a dream.

Feelings Could Change

I've found worth in your presence, priceless.
I cherish your words of admiration,
They follow me like curious puppies.
And though I don't yet love you,
It's still very possible these feelings
Could change into such beautiful butterflies.

Get a Room You Two

Evergreen, aqua blue butterflies rest
On top of the tangerine shed outside.
They stare so deeply into each other's eyes
That they both drown...

Firefly

She loved pillow
Talks but only if they
Were worth their weight in gold.

I asked how can a sound
Represent colour?

Her wink whispered, "You'll see."

I can tell you're on another level
Looking down, and I'm not good with heights
But I do like being high.

I get that a lot hangin' out with you along
These endless, random roads.

And at midnight in our secret spot,
The fireflies come out to play,
And we glow brighter than all of them.

Insert Love Story

Ever so silently, she weaves her web,
Waiting close by her trap, she can wait all day.
She's confident a moth or a firefly
Will stop on by for the first and last time.
She's waiting for her one-night stand,
Then she'll eat him after if she loves him.
She will, tasty kill in her mind,
No point in wasting food,
Especially after the day she's had.
Pretty little Black Widow,
Beautiful and a ghost.
She said, "Leave while you still can, my pet."
He whispered, "Soulmate?"
She laughed, and said,
"I can't wait to drain you of existence."

The Last of You

You're caught in a web, fly.
Pay no attention to these fangs;
They are harmless till I drive
Them into your skin like nails into pine.
You should know, I will drain
You of all essence,
To further my own existence
As I lay another one to waste,
Tasting the last of you
Like it's the last thing I'll ever taste.

From Spider to Fly

I found you in a moment of weakness.
I found you in my cross hairs, dead to rights.
You will help me survive, I will eat you alive.
You will be mine for the first time, for the last time.

Honeybee

At first, I thought you
Were a queen bee, but
You weren't put here to multiply.

You were always a honeybee,
And I loved what you made
From your mind,
The sweetness of your genius,
Undeniable soothing light.

You may still be a honeybee,
And I might be allergic to your weapon,
But if it meant staying or leaving
You behind
I'd rather risk
Getting stung,
As fatal as this all
Could become.

I'd risk it all just to hold
You every once in a while,
'Cause your energy
Feels better than anything.

Bumbles

Bumbles bounce around
The yard from flower to flower
Doing what bumbles do best.
They sure are cute and fuzzy.
Just don't sting me and the yard is yours.

When Honey Dances

When honey dances, it moves with such effortless grace.
It is like a lonely siren in the sea.
The honey speaks to me without voice.
Such a delicious experience, such a fine thing.
The honey is full of sorrow.
Long are the days of old when honey belonged
To the bees, now torn away.
What profound knowledge is stored within
Its mysterious glow?
It is the knowledge of the bees.
It is like a swirling ballerina dressed in neon lights.
It dances for all of us.

Scorpions

With a tail of death, you silently wait for
The perfect time to strike poison into your prey,
So quick on the draw and beautiful in design.
A reminder to tread carefully when walking in
The world or suffer great injury you'll never forget.

The Gospel According to a Sparrow

Feathered wonders rest
On a ruby-bricked wall,
And sing to their maker,
"Thank you."
I say it back and smile.
This is the gospel according
To a sparrow,
Where did you fly off to?
I missed your energy,
Your commentary
On life as it happens.
I know you're only doing
Your best to live
A life devoted to
Someone you cannot
See in the flesh,
But they say He is coming
Back soon, get ready.
It will be sudden and final.

A Blue Jay's Song

You migrated to an excellent location,
Setting up home next to the ocean.
You've always been loved, even in times of war.
Now you sit calmly,
On the beach with your own additions,
With two new souls to share moments.
I'm grateful they keep you smiling.
I'm proud of your resilience.
And should I exit this show and tell before you,
Know I'll do my best to watch over you
From the realm of light,
Still writing lyrics to a blue jay's song.

Robin on the Fence

As you shoot off into the sky
To star in a new chapter in your life's movie,
Remember to use your gentle heart
That runs like a river.
It's what got you this far,
And it'll carry you further down
All roads, down the roads you will
Travel to when I stop churning out poems
And breathe out my last exhale.
I'm so very proud of all that you've accomplished,
With the time given to you.
I love you mountain climber,
Danger facer, robin on the fence
Of all I've ever known.

Barn Owls

Night watchman, hidden above the world
In treetops, in search of another victim.
Oh the mice fear and hate you so, but I admire
Your work in the nighttime glow.
You are artwork brought to life in search of life to take.
I want to age and vanish like your complexion.

Hercinia

Deep in the haunted forests,
High in their branches,
It glows with a holy presence.
On nights like these
We would be lost
If not for its
Light, guiding us along.
Deep in the chambers of our troubled
Hearts, we have always known
You were there.
Hercinia, guide us all home.

Battle Cat

Behold, a superior model.
Feast your eyes upon a legendary planet.
It is a mighty beast, a rogue, a machine.
Behold the noble Battle Cat.
Defiler of fridges,
And guardian of a far-off land,
Where imagination runs wild
Like the Saskatchewan River.

Panda Transmissions

You and I are two pandas in a tree kissing.
We cause havoc to this poor world.
She never had a chance or saw us coming.
I've been sending transmissions to your heart,
So you're never too far from mine.

The Guide

A blur of red and white,
Blood and teeth hiding
The presence of a fox tonight.
I noticed him making a kill.
He looked back as if to say,
"What thrills you bores me, so
Stay present, remain still."
Was it you who mourned for sunlight?
I might've been lost forever out here without
Your guiding footsteps.
So, I will lift my torch and follow.
Lead me out of this forest and
Back to the main road.

Fox Chase

There I go, off chasing the fox
Who's after the hens again.
She makes quick work of lush forest.
It seems I'll never have what it takes
To find middle ground.
There she goes down the tunnels of tomorrow.
All I ever catch is just a glimpse of her tail
Waving goodbye.

We Call Him Tedders

My heart lays sleeping upstairs.
Sleep, you furry little thing.
Dream of playing fetch for infinity.
And while you do, I'll keep watch over you,
So you can live, continue to be that
Adorable bundle of joy,
You've always been.

Furry Little Terror

You, little terror, you
Are made of love, and are my friend
After a tough day at work,
With the constant desire to play.
You light me up every time
I see you; you keep a smile
On my face, little angel of light.

A Wolf in a Tuxedo

I left the pack and came alone tonight
As a wolf in a tuxedo,
But don't let these filthy clothes fool you, love;
I am starving, anxious, and I haven't written in days.
But when I take the time to pick up
A pen, something happens.
Now, throw ink down, fill up this page please.
But wolves don't write; they bite the jugular.
Tonight, compels me to do both.

Revenge of the Wild

Lone wolf wandering the windy path,
The same route your old pack would go
On a mission, blood on their lips from a fresh kill.
And a smile that caused them all to howl
At the moon, wild till the day they died.
It was man who separated you between worlds.
His instrument of death thundered.
And then the love of your life fell silent to the earth,
Never to rise again.
But you escaped, remembering his scent,
And have now found him asleep in his tent.
Before you sank your teeth into him
You howled, "This is revenge of the wild."

War Horse

I painted a war horse over my bed tonight.
So I can keep on riding armed
To the teeth in dreams where the light
Is always the farthest thing away.
Where it's impossible to make sense of the grey.
I created a war horse for you to ride on into the sunset with,
Where the good guy always gets the girl and the villain's
billions.
On these war horses I've chosen to carry on the message.
And the sound of heavy hoofs
Ripping up the ground always gets my blood going.
Tonight makes me wonder if you're still up there.
War horse, do you see everything wrong with the world?
Do you see everything wrong with me?

The Stallion

As I passed by the ocean
And made my way down miles of road,
I saw a beautiful horse-drawn carriage.
Those inside couldn't hide their smiles.
The winter-white stallion was massive,
Able to carry the weight for hours.
Part of me was happy just to see him on
His merry way, the other part wanted
To see him run free from his obligations.

Zebra

I'm a rabies-infected stallion,
Wild and divided.
I'm a skull, white and black-hole dark.
I'm an eye sore and a work of art.
I'm a zebra split down the centre.
I'm a sinner, a saint and a ghost.

Now Crimson

Take it back,
Swallow your words
While you heinously spit tar
At blinking stars.
Like devious lions feasting
On a fresh kill,
Shamelessly parading
Their pearly white fangs,
Now crimson.

Primal

I hear my twenty-three-year-old voice in my dreams,
Where I'm living like I used to, wild, random, reckless and rude.
I ran in the streets till dawn, hearing seagulls squawking
At me, I returned fire with raised middle fingers.
The fiery eagle of my youth soared beyond space and time.
It went into hiding and emerged a Siberian tiger.
Deadly and primal.

Battle Tigers

Giant armoured battle tigers
Are appearing from dreams to waking world streets.
They're painting everything crimson,
Slaughtering anything with a pulse,
And I can't help but smile at the loss of my enemies.

Just Another Day

Winter is one with Siberian tigers hunting.
Everything screams designed for this,
Perfect alpha creatures,
As the deer is torn to ribbons, you feast.
I'm thankful for distance,
'Cause it's just another day for the king.

Mei

Giant beast,
So precious, and part of a rare breed.
Intelligent, and formidable,
Swaying your mighty trunk to and fro.
You roam the jungle with a caring heart.
I hope you enjoy your life until you depart.

Arctic Cookie Star

Tiny arms open like
A door mat that eats sponges.
I'll leave you here, for other
Divers to find and snap pictures of,
Precious jewels of the sea,
Attached to this underwater city.

Vampire Squid

Underwater, deep below,
You haunt the ocean with your presence,
Menacing yet beautiful.
Well, this is the place we go when
We want to be bewildered, and it shows.
Your eyes glow like a constellation, like the moon.
I swear you move just like a specter.

Man of War

I drew breath and exhaled
You like a sad poem.
With a crushed heart
In my chest and
A broken promise
Still playing back on my mind.
I thought I was above
These stinging man of war tentacles
Reaching out at my ankles.

Deep Sea Divin'

Deep sea dive with me.
We'll take a submarine down
As far as we can go.
I'm in it to see monsters,
New breeds of weird and wild.
I'm in it to see the look on your face
When we discover Megalodons
Lurking beneath us smiling.

Kissing a Cobra

Poison running off her tongue,
Her kisses are lethal.
She's blood drunk, and talented.

She hissed,
"How will you ever
Get your life back after this fall?

You're just another one turning blue,
Convulsing on the floor.

Oh, how will you ever
Live your life fearless
Like before?"

Gustave

Supposedly, the legend goes,
That you're responsible
For three hundred dead.
So they say.
But you've lost count,
Bullets bounced right off your armour,
Spears didn't stop you, they failed.
You're a dragon swimming
In the water, smiling
And whispering,
"I'm always hungry, so
I'll haunt the river,
Feasting on flesh for as long as I like."

Utah Raptors

They gathered in the dense forests,
Had the scent of a victim,
Screeched a game plan,
And how quickly they surrounded the unexpected,
How fiercely they slashed it to pieces,
And started feasting on it alive, raw and bloody
Until it was just a mangled corpse.
The leader of the pack shrieked,
"The scavengers
Can have what's left of you.
We won't stop with one,
We're not even close to being done.
Tonight, we'll kill another just for fun.
We'll carve up your loved ones with our weapons
As your flesh gets stripped right off the bones.
Talons and jaws around your throat.
Oh, here we go, jugular ripped out.
The end of your reign was tasty."

T-Rex

You were the boss, sitting on
Your throne, only leaving it to
Make quick work of the prey before you.
Your legend and reign passed through the ages.
You hunted with binocular vision and
An enhanced sense of smell.
Once something was in your crosshairs,
There was little they could do to escape
Your razor teeth and bite force.
You would crush bones and smile,
As you ripped out chunks of flesh
Like a proper prehistoric king.

Enigma

Into the deep lurks mythical sea creatures,
With shining lights, extensions of themselves,
Reflections of hellish beasts on Earth.
And no one knows how many live below
Where the sun won't go.
No one knows how much I have in common
With icebergs these days.
Into deep territory, I've come face to face
With my inner animal.
And it has no name except enigma.

My Guardian Angel

He uttered to himself,
"I'm giving up the chase;
For once, love, chase me.
And if you catch me, kiss me.
And if you miss me, move on.
I knew about your condition,
Didn't scare me away, did it?
My guardian angel keeps me grounded."
He said, "I'm not here to love
The past you,
So let's start this whole thing off
Brand new to the senses."

Neon Thunderstorm

I used to dream about you in summer;
You'd enter and exit my life like a neon
Thunderstorm where rain and hail felt like daggers.
And in that place, I'd chase after you, as you disappeared
With the fog.
I could hear your laugh as you kept running farther away.
You wouldn't even look back,
You couldn't see my tears follow me from dream to waking day.

Gnomes

There you are.
Just look at you,
Puffing away on your wooden pipe,
Deep in contemplation
Of the universe, and all things wise.
Look at you atop your mushroom kingdom.
"This is all mine for all time!"
Says the Gnome.
"Soon my friends will come and join me for tea.
Soon we will speak of eternity and ecstasy.
Soon we will see beyond our vision."

Lit

The gnome said to me
"In the garden I was lit
Like five hundred thousand torches
Dying to spit illumination.
In the garden, did I sit.
My mind in motion
Making as much sense as I could ever get
Being poisoned, meditating
Till I knew what fit
And what was meant to be discarded.
There I saw everything melt and blend,
Colours woven into my head.
And even when my eyes were closed,
I could see them,
Spinning and shining.
Unapologetically
Screaming
"This circus is really happening!"

Judging Eyes

Throughout the garden and the yard,
Live mischievous gnomes sitting on giant mushrooms.
Smoking pipes, guarding the flowers with judging eyes.
Always watching, judging, and high as the planets in space.

Space Moth

Oh, mighty wings spread out
To sail into another galaxy.
Home is wherever I go
Piloting the space moth.

If you won't let me in
I will continue alone,
And not give a damn,
And not feel a thing,
Not one shred of remorse.
I will press on in search
Of a suitable replacement.

See, I can find in her
What I found in you.
And you should know, I will.

Like Flying Vikings

Get aboard this wild ride.
Off we go into space
Armed with lightning swords,
Shields, and battle axes.
Off we go to chase demons
And pillage planets tenfold.
Off we go to journey the stars
And live by the sounds of ancient
Behemoth noises.
With enemy blood
On our tongues and
Food in our bellies,
Off to face the next foe
We sail, cursed and eternal.

Rotation

Over the white noise,
I hear her under a blood moon,
My tornado spinning outta control
Searching for a new note in a wall of sound.
What do I do with my anxiety
Eating away at me like acid rain?
Help me get there, Father.
Does it bother you, that I'm not there yet?
You know, you're on heavy rotation in my head,
Like super cars on a racetrack,
With stars that match your eyes in the dark.

I'll Bring You Back Moonrocks

Hello space suit,
Lift off, here we go,
Precious moon,
Goodbye gravity.
We are officially a world away
From home, look at her spin
Like the miracle planet she is.
I'll bring you back moonrocks,
I promise.

Closer to the Moon than to Me

I'm racing towards the light,
Like a bullet train, en route to your mind.
It's okay; I am more than my birthday's snow and ice.
I came into this world like you did,
With a broken cry.
But I am not your continuation.
And I'm not channelling your energy;
I've got my own design.
You said in a dream,
"You'll join the red and white starlight sky someday,
Closer to the moon than to me."

Only Golden Artist

After the clock has struck the end of my watch,
I peace out.
And baby If you have green eyes,
You have my utmost attention.
You've got all of me now.
If you're a stunner, you get all that I can give.
Love stories I'll never write about,
Bite marks that scar,
Phantom kisses in the dark.
I would destroy a million worlds
To be your only golden artist....

Worlds Together

Last night I met a new warm soul.
I felt a spark and connection.
Last night, I witnessed a sample of her heart
And realized that I wanted more.
I want to know you stranger,
And I will follow my intuition
As far as it may lead me,
And whether it ends before it begins
Or suddenly ends like a heart attack,
I will stand still,
Waiting to bring our damaged worlds together.

Free Trips

When I look into your soul gates,
I leave Earth, take off, and go up to
Cloud level to see
Your eyes like scorching asteroids
Headed for my home.
They disarm me and kill me at
The same time.
What's the point of paying to
Go to Mars, when
I have free trips off world
Just by kissing you good night.

Aurora Borealis

What'll change in these next few days?
I dunno, we'll see;
Maybe we'll be more,
Or inevitably stay as strangers.
'Cause you should know,
I can live with either answer.
Blue diamond,
You are what men sell their souls for.
Maybe God will grant us our own
Audience of aurora borealis tonight.
But I don't have to count
On the sky to find them;
I see them in your
Supernatural crosshairs
And I know they have power over me—
My Lord, do they ever.
You whispered, "Surrender,"
As a shooting star went by,
Followed suddenly by an army of angels.
I saw you among them,
Dressed in light.

I Wish It Was You

I only see one star tonight.
I wish it was you advertising your love
And light to that sick street downtown.
Which side will you take
When the time comes to be cannibal?
I only see one star tonight
And even if it's not you,
it's the most I've felt
About anything in the last five years.

Red and White Starlight Sky

I see constellations of fire in your crosshairs,
Reflections of a red and white starlight sky in your design.
You speak like deep space tonight,
With words like asteroids and meteors in my mind.
You stare right through my layers to my heart,
Blazing like the sun into my life, into my very soul
Until I fly in dreams just like you move in the waking day.

Constellation

Shine on precious jewel;
Look at you glow angel.
Your wings are showing,
And that smile goes for miles.
Look at you glow in the dark pink diamond light.
Look at you grow as an individual.
Across the constellation of your eyes,
I'm there waiting for them to find me.

Space

For everything I am,
I'm so much more alive when I'm beside you.
You're my own personal universe of healing;
You're a brand new sun,
And the stars' inspiration to become
Giant shimmering diamonds.
I close my eyes and picture your face,
Your smile, your laugh,
And I'm high from the thought of them.
I will meet you on the other side
Of consciousness tonight;
We'll surf through space
Till we find a new planet
To share the warmth.

Brand New Earth

We stepped off the face
Of the planet entirely,
Suddenly weightless,
Priceless and free
As a golden eagle in the sky.
Look at us above giants;
Look at us being satellites.
You did this on purpose;
You made me obsessed with
Jotting life down in sentences
The best I can in the moments I'm given.
I turned to you and suddenly
Nothing else mattered
Besides making it into Heaven.
I wanna drink from the river of life
And walk with you through green pastures
Looking at all your creations.
I wanna walk with you, Lord, to learn
The secrets of the universe,
For infinity on a brand new Earth.

The City of Love

I foresee myself on a long dark road, with a backpack full of
Empty pages, a stash of pens, a provocative cologne and
A green tea to fight off the bitter cold of night's attack.
I'm fighting off the teeth and claws of October.
I'm fighting off the memories of those that once were,
For they are no longer here;
They are there underneath slabs of rock,
Underneath the land we take for granted.
I foresee coffee and a cute little dame to love into the night's
waves.
And who's to say that I'll ever truly fall in love; I'll probably
just fall in lust.
And maybe that'll be enough.
Maybe I don't need a ring, maybe that time has passed.
Maybe all I need is a wild dreamy night every so often to keep
This old dog still alive.
Will God say, "You are forgiven for giving her all you had"?
"Come with us son, to the city of love beyond the stars,
To one day take charge of your own planet that burns a
trillion times
More brilliant than Mars."

Come Out Sunlight

Come out sunlight.
Farewell for now, dear old moon.
The day has just begun burning anew,
And night will be here very soon.
I want to be there,
To hold your hand, be your man,
But I'm stuck in a haunted place,
And the only way out is to bring everything down.

Red and White Starlight Sky (Part 2)

Somehow, I survived the dangers of
Your red and white starlight sky.
I wonder if I'll radiate now after
Surviving the meteor shower from your mouth,
That went off like a machine gun
Into the deepest parts of my essence.
I've tried to keep my centre pure,
To only burn what doesn't feel right,
But I'm stuck in a world of broken
Glass and promises.

You Shine the Brightest

Bleach white roses woven into musical notes.
Cherry-flavoured letters addressed to a goddess.
How sweet you truly are, beyond all measure, beyond
All stars; you shine the brightest in the galaxy.

You're a Galaxy to Me

I'm trying this new door; I'm taking this last
Chance to see where it leads, to see if she's behind it.
There you are love!
Smile, silence, awkward pause.
Staring up in search of battle angels,
Blowing trumpets out of the clouds.
Invisible gates open;
We need this. Don't you see we need this?
Miracle come down.
Stretches forever, it stretches forever, you should see it.
And even if you do, you're only seeing a fraction, of a
Fraction, of a fraction of.... this just goes on...
...Of a fraction, of a fraction, of a fraction of one
Galaxy out of this universe of healing.
Don't look this way.
Please don't look this way, I'm not ready
To hear what you're about to tell me.
Wasting away, self-loathing,
Wasting away.
Will you try me?
Will you be my heaven until then?
Just one kiss to tide me over and prolong my life.
Just one last chance to prove my worth in something.
You're a galaxy to me.

Forever Red and White

They're planets singing in the space inside my mind.
They're supernovas exploding at the thought of finding
True love, at the possibility of living my dreams.
And I still want them, I still want this sand through my hands
To let me hold it for a moment longer.
And the stars dancing in my eyes are forever red and white.
The meteor showers rain at night as my heavy eyelids close,
But not for good.
It's difficult to sleep lately knowing you no longer need to.

Meteor Shower

Light up the night, darling phoenix.
"Vengeance," she said,
Screaming ultraviolet rays.
I will remedy this situation,
Assess the damage
Done within and
Prepare to rebuild.
Restart your castle;
You're gonna need to start over
If you survive the meteor shower
From my mouth.

Fire Angel

I was smoking a cigar
When I saw this fire angel fall
From the sky like a meteor shower.
I followed the trail she left behind,
Her footprints tattooed into the ground.
Angel of wrath and flame,
Your eyes, focused on the supernatural
Mission at hand that
You will complete before
Heaven calls you home again.

The Abandoned One

I went walking down by the river
Last night to find myself
Drinking in starlight.
I found a busted-up angel
Crying and rocking back and forth.
Why so sad love?
Why the tears?
She said I can't help it;
I used to sing in Heaven
Now I'm down here in hell.
Oh, I've damned myself
And no one can save me.
You've got it all wrong, you are paradise.
It's nights like this one
That save our souls.
Won't you walk with me?
I promise not to leave your side
Until you return to the sky.

Warmth

You ignite a flame dead centre and
It's outta my hands now; these feelings
Fall like leaves around me silently.
Autumn is like a kiss goodbye
From the love song that
Is summer; I miss its music already.
Maybe we'll fall so madly in love,
Or maybe we'll fall away
From each other's warmth.
'Cause it feels like I'm sitting next to a campfire
When you're around.

I Was the Fire

As a boy, I'd often dream about
Rushing into burning buildings, axe in hand
Ready to save those in need from their end.
Always, just in time.
As a man, I realized I had it all wrong.
I was no savior; I was the fire.

Flames Behind My Eyes

There is chaos within me that no one can see.
Each moment, regardless of being awake or asleep,
Feeds this machine.
I tried to warn you to stay distant,
'Cause you can get third degree burns from my carnage.
I throw everything I am into these flames behind my eyes;
Everything I have goes in there.

Torches

Like two torches
That hide wisdom inside,
You winked at me and I turned bright red.
Oh, you're all the things
I dream about.
Winter rose,
You're a phoenix
In early autumn.
I'm addicted to your glowing smile,
Like an angel in the flesh,
Like a model who stepped
Off the runway for a while to catch her breath.

House Fire

You ran back into the house
To save the fire,
Crazy as hell, but you didn't
Say why you thought the flames
Were dear friends until you were burnt.
Until they hurt you.
No one told you the rules, just woke up
And ran with anxiety and
Rain showering the city.
Every drop drove you mad.

Hold Steady

Hold steady,
The sea stirs this night,
Storm is coming, aye,
'Tis only a matter of time
Till she takes us below.
'Tis only a fool's paradise.
The Kraken will try to
Drag us all down so
Arm yourselves men.
'Tis the devil's work
Reaching up at our ankles!
Get us out of these waters
Least it comes to take
Us straight to hell with a smile!

Cobalt

Cobalt for miles.
Somehow, I'm not sick.
I'll be sticking with what I know about distance,
And how it heals my battle-scarred soul.
I'm on top of this boat sailing
With the fresh smell of salt and the wind
At my back, the world in front of me.
With open arms waiting for me to reach land,
Saying "You belong here son, stay as long as you want.
Stay as long as you can."

Every Mile Away from You

Looking out into the night
From a ship sailing the Atlantic.
They told me they found
The ghost of you, once forgotten.
So on I sail through this ancient divide,
In search of finding a new place to start over.
And every mile away from you,
Every single mile heals me more
Than I ever was before.
And every mile away from you fixes me.

Sleep on It

For all our faults,
We match perfectly.
For all our differences,
We belong together
Like the wings on a dove.
Like a storm at sea.
Like beating hearts in bodies.
Like the loyalty of a dog.
Like the rebirth every morning.
Like the faith of a born-again believer.
Like a bookshelf just for me.
Like burning rubber on 8th street.
Like leaving a legacy.
Sleep on it,
While I work.

April Model

There she goes, April model,
Welcome to a new world
Beyond the bottle.
I'm trying make something
Of myself fast,
Better leave the past
Like a ship casting off,
And move like a wild cat
Away from the source
Of all my problems.

Fluffy Bright Clouds

Fluffy bright clouds,
Over heavenly fields where my dreams
Take me for adventures into the unknown.
I sit cross-legged underneath this utopian sky
As waves of colour rekindle my soul's flaming phoenix
In the dying hours of July.
This summer has helped treat injury
With love and understanding.
Let's drink to our buzzing bumble bee agendas.
Sit down, stay a while; raindrops are inbound.
I want to relive this one moment
As many times as memory will allow.
I want to remember that this valley of anything is possible
And bring its guiding light into my tomorrow.

She Brings the Clouds to You

I found peace in a new song on repeat.
I found a new pretend
Where I was always on
The side of sunshine.
I could never be in the wrong
As long as I played that song.
The way she carries herself,
She doesn't need any help to
Bring you to clouds.
She brings the clouds to you.

I Wish I Was That Mountain

We're so close to land
And past the shoreline,
There are mountains.

We're so far from comfort
But all I can think of is
This moment suspended over water.

But right now my heart
Is exploring new places.

And there are mountains kissing clouds.

I wish I was that mountain.
I wish those clouds were the lips
Of the one that got away.

Kenopsia

I've seen this place go from
Beehive to ghost town.
I've noticed the tumbleweeds pass by
Silently, drifters in the wind,
And here comes the harmless army, at it again.
I was a lesser man when I first got here;
Now the momentum is with me
And I can't stop it.
I think I stole it from
Where it all started.

Tuesday

Sitting on a milk chocolate couch,
Surrounded by pictures of rainbow sketches on black paper.

The grinning cat's eyes move back and forth
In sync with the ticking of the clock's hands,
Constantly staring me down.

On my left, a well-used record player
And an impressive collection.
And on and on it plays into the years to come.

I'm enjoying Tuesday with a friend;
We're just two souls lost in the blur and static.

Lost in the Static

Dang it frost, dang it Jack.
Why'd ya have ta be like that?
Say I'm sorry I should have had your back.
It must be this way, lost in the static.

Does It Still Hold True?

The phone rings and I refuse to answer.
The music flows and I don't move.
My mind dances and I follow its destination.
I'm searching for a way through fog and mystery this year.
Here's crossin' ma fingers, remembering the ghost's words.
"To find peace you need not search any further than yourself.
For within is the gift I've given you, since before you were born.
Remember my sacrifice and what you said you once believed in.
Does it still hold true?"

My Beautiful Friend

There's a goddess in another city, an angel,
Who knows how to heal my soul.
A few moments with my beautiful friend
Makes me strong enough to take on the world again.
She's a rare diamond who keeps me going
When the path is uphill.
She pushes me to dig in deep and climb.

Lava Lamp

I love the vibes you're
Emitting like a bright blue lava lamp.
Maybe if I look at you as my potential wife,
And not another muse,
Things will go that direction.

All I Ask

There are no more lights,
So I'll say this in the dark in silence.
If I am to be tested, allow me a clear path,
For I cannot falter if doubt is a word I don't know.
Knowledge is every direction.
And all I ask; is you point me to mine.

Recycling the Glass

On my wall hangs a ruby-eyed vigilante, a skull
With roses, and a gnome smoking a pipe
Sitting on a giant mushroom.

On my wall hangs a list of titles
I hope to turn into books.
I can't seem to remember them all,
So I wrote them down.

I'll capture lightning in bottles.
I'll recycle the glass,
And keep the words for myself.

Dying Trend

My dreams are stronger lately,
For visions of Heaven no longer seem unreachable.
Indicate you understand; we're going there soon.
We'll replace snow for sand as I
Decimate birthday candles, wishing
For my own star.
Nothing I can't handle.
In time my friend this dying trend
Will take us all to better days
Filled completely with disbelief.
I'll remember your kind heart
Was never too far from reach.

Saddest Woman I Know

There you go, stealing my last chance at finding hope.
You drifted off towards the stars in search of the unknown.
There you go, eating my heart like an apple.
There you go on your own,
Living life as the saddest woman I know.

Third Level Window

From the third level window looking down
At all the glow from the highs and lows
Of this live movie in the front yard,
I know they'll make their way to the streets to tango.
I know they're off to take adventures,
Make memories and learn lessons.
They're off to enjoy the show.
I want to take a shot of tequila and an espresso,
And open the door to the unknown
World waiting outside for me.

Like Whoa

Sometimes words back flip off my tongue
Into your ears.
Sometimes you don't even
Notice me talking,
I'm simply not there, but
Quite often
I spit supernova explosions.
I release magma,
Liquid metal.
Quite often I come here
To this place of confession.
Like whoa, it was you that let me down,
Better to walk out of my life than stick around.

I Never Let You In

I kept you alive in my mind all these years,
Where you sat by rivers meditating,
Trying to restore what was taken,
Trying to save your soul
In the confines of daylight.
And when night happens,
I let you go flame on like a firefly,
Trying to consume what's bright,
Trying to fly away from this life.
I never let you in,
I never let you into mine,
But I always hoped someday I might.

Mortals

You rise from my dreams,
Splash reality with kisses on my forehead.
I wake up to sparrows singing songs.
I roll out of bed with your colours and language
Still at the back of my mind.
I'm still wiping away dreams from my eyes,
And trying to focus, like you wouldn't believe but
You remind me, I'm only mortal.
And mortals weren't meant to love angels.

Electric Summer Drive

Electric summer drive,
Off-road into the elements,
Witness to salmon-coloured petals falling
Silently from great branches like green anacondas
Reaching up searching for God.
Past landmarks forgotten, known only by me
And a couple friends
Who write to keep ourselves sane,
Living off black coffee and apple pie.
This planet is full of hungry animals
In this circus around me, this jungle, this forest,
This untamed land I drive to time and time again.
Have I gone mad for loving almost all creatures?
Whose features strike like lightning bolts upon my senses.
I dreamed this day would come to life,
I dreamed it into existence tonight.

All I Want Today

All I want today is to enjoy the sun,
Remind someone they are loved,
And feel the ice thaw off my heart.
All I want today is to live honestly.

Jack-In-The-Box

I am just a witness to majestic wings
Carved outta bones.
Made for strangers' eyes to keep and to hold.
My eyes have held enough weight, waiting for
The climax of tonight to spring like a jack-in-the-box
And overtake my senses.

Sponge

I soaked up your words, let them fill my mind.
With your best friend gone now, what fills the void?
What in all the world could ever fill that hole in your chest?
I hope you find solace in these words
For they're all I can offer.
I don't know to a certainty just how far
Down you've fallen,
Just as you cannot possibly fathom the depths of my curse
Without being in my shoes.
And maybe it's better off this way, maybe it's safer
Locking up the monsters inside us that only
Want to break free and wreak havoc in the night.

Serpentine

Spirit warrior riding a flaming demon horse.
Breath visible.
Blue flames burning bright.
Leaving living pictures in my mind.
Serpentine dreams swallowing me whole tonight.

How Deep

Who else but you could bring me out of death country?
Who else but you could steal my heart with a kiss and a smile?
I waited for you while the waves crashed against the boat;
They reminded me of how deep your beauty went.
And even dead centre, beneath the skin,
You were always a brilliant glowing angel.
How deep your beauty went; it pulled me in like a portal
To the next life.

Quicksand

If this is the last time
We'll see each other,
You should know your presence
Can't be replaced.
We both tried and, in the end,
The result was fated,
While we waited
For God to show us how to live.
We got so incredibly lost
And I thought the cost was too much
To pay, but I was just sinking anyway
Until he saved me.

Mesmerized

In between breath,
I drift off and think of her
Creating another masterpiece,
And how she is a masterpiece
That I would love to wake up to every morning.
In between thought
She floods my brain.
Every time I see her
I forget my surroundings.
I forget she's not mine.

Anti-Hero

Man, sometimes life feels like an incredibly bad trip,
And son, I pinch myself often,
But I don't wake up and then I say colourful words and turn
Bright red because sometimes I don't wanna be here.
I'd trade places with you stranger instead.
But I won't.
I'll just keep being an anti-hero waiting for the snow
To cover my tracks as I trek on down miles
And miles of uncharted road.
I wish you were still here,
And that tomorrow wasn't
Related to today.

The Next Time

Act like the tiger you are inside.
Don't worry 'bout "What if
I go for their jugular?"
You will.
Feast on the bounty before
Your alpha eyes.
Remember we all go to a far-off place,
And we never come back the same.
And we fail to remember our names,
Till the next time we open our minds.

Sons of the Night

We went into the night with nothing
Planned and everything to gain.
Nothing, but the good old taste
Of tea to hold us together.
We went right into the night,
And I said, "Eat your heart out Toon town!"
I will not live here forever so I'm enjoying what I can,
While I can, with whoever I can.
Thank you, friends,
For joining the journey with me thus far.
You hold me together with your
Platonic tar and I confess I am truly a mess
But I'll save the best for a chosen few,
For we are the sons of the night;
We are no one's muse but our own.

Dinner Date

He sat waiting for her at the
Diner overlooking the river,
With the bridge dressed in lights,
The stars above shinning brilliantly,
Candles, wine, and Vietnamese cuisine.
As he breathed in the aromas of this sleepy city,
The one he had always called home,
Suddenly, it felt like a stranger to him,
And he didn't know why.
He didn't know why this one dreamy night
Out of all the others was so different.
Then he realized the obvious
Had been eluding him, he was in love.
She was his other, or so he thought.
He needed to be lifted and move on
Down the roads of time.
She would be here in ten minutes
To ring in the new year in style.

You Were Here First

I keep hearing that sarcastic voice of the past saying
"Oh, good job, you're a rock star now, you're a monk,
Philosopher Joe schmoe, Zen poet, heartbreaking one.
Wild travelling carnival of words."
But those titles no longer define me these days.
You were here first; I can't take any credit.

Lens

Bended metal covers the wall like skin,
Of birds, acorns and tar colour.
I can relate;
I was once a satellite sending out
Transmissions of pain and regret,
Of anger and sadness
Before you entered my life.
Only now does the camera change its lens.

Remind Myself

I could write a book of sorrow too;
It could be the best thing I ever do.
And I'll remind myself,
This is the only way I'll ever have you.

Instinct

It used to be that every two weeks I'd drive my grandpa's
Dreams around the city.
Now I just sit in coffee shops and spill my guts over pages.
Someone told me the night is young and you're so beautiful
And they were right.
What can I say to convince you I'm not a Doberman or a thug?
What can I do to break the silence, for you are a goddess and a man
Can only be destroyed so many times.
I know how to save you from what haunts, because your life
Doesn't make sense right now.
So, listen to your instincts or you'll never know the meaning
Behind your heartbeat.

Journey

Hover over and breathe in the crystal kingdom,
'Cause I could be gone by the time you read this.
I may have travelled on
In search of a new home world,
At the other end of space,
To escape the way you made me
Forget I was alive.

I've travelled around the sun
And felt the spin of a thousand miles an hour.
Every other face I know is happy on the outside,
But inside they're just dying stars.

I could be the same as you
And you'd never know it by the way I look.
I keep myself, to myself
In the hopes that I don't push you away
'Cause I can be corrosive.

I can be everything warm you need,
A passing by meteor shower.
I can be starlight.
I can be a refreshing breeze when you're suffocating
In a dark moment some night.

I can be more; I can be precious memories that take you back
To your grandparents, or
Your so-called once upon a time best friend, maybe
The love of your life you still punish yourself
Trying not to think about.

I could be so many things
But I'm not even one of your reflections.
No radio waves of yours wonder about mine.
And that's okay.
I've found an alternative way to survive.

I follow the rivers in the off season.
I follow the canyons till I reach the end of the path,
Where I leave parts of myself behind, a frozen recorded
Soul dancing my own dance to the style I choose to keep
under mask,
Until Friday night lights hit me like thunder bolts.

Ancient Rome

I'm taking over the wheel as
I steal what I can from my dreams
And bring them into the light,
Just like you bring me to life.
Being near you makes me feel like
I've conquered Ancient Rome.

In The Dying Light

In the dying light I write to clear these cobwebs,
To clear away all veils, to fight back and return the favour.
Streetlamps illuminate houses,
And melted snowbanks shine like diamonds.
At my centre, I am ice.
I hope the truce will hold.
Let's go long into the night and stir
The other realm, the city beyond shadows.
You're a part of this world, just not a part of mine.
You dig and stab and bite at my heart all the time.
I don't need to kill your memory;
It's already dead to me—see, you're blind.
You try too hard and not enough.
And do what? And go where?
Only you can answer these questions.

Who Knows?

Let's hop in your ride and away we go, man,
Onwards towards the sunset and then the endless
Sky of stars awaits us.
And then who knows what's
Around the corner, who knows, man.
Maybe it's someone new to love.
Maybe it's salvation.
Maybe it's the end.

Ready To Bounce?

I've got everything we'll need
For the next four months.
Can't wait to pet the pandas.
I wanna take one home,
I can't help it,
I can't wait to feed the crocodiles,
Those cold-blooded apex predators.
I can't wait to swim to shore and
Kiss the sandy beaches, like I made it home
Thank God!
I can't wait to get away
From the only place I ever seem to go.

Waiting to Take Your Own Hand Home

Whatever transpires tonight
Might be the reason for leaving this town. Just fly,
Never look back, join the sky.
That's what she said
And I never meant
To be a part of this failure.
Would you cross the oceans to find yourself
Waiting to take your own hand home?

Invincible

I tune out the world when it's crowded,
When I should speak,
When you walk into the room.
Everything around me, neglected;
I want only you.
Maybe they were right; maybe I'm a fool
For the impossible,
Who's falling hard from way up here,
But I'm bound for Earth soon.
It's quiet, and it's killing
Me 'cause your voice is all I need
To be invincible.

The Calm Morning Water

I cast out my line upon the calm
Morning water, as a loon calls for his other
To join in the crisp Albertan air.
I take note of his call and smile
As I slowly reel in my lure,
And cast off once again in another direction.
There's something about this that reanimates my centre.
There was something about her
That won't disappear no matter
How much time passes.
I wish you were still single, butterfly,
And we were playing board games
And sitting next to the campfire.
You could've been my heart's lullaby.

I'll Put in a Good Word for Ya

These days, it's hard to tell
Who's a trusting pair of listening ears,
Or a careless pair of loose lips.
Because I know someone who does
More than just sink ships; she burns
Cities to the ground in nuclear waves
Every time she opens her mouth.

Sped Fast

Sped fast into the nakedness
Of night, a ship through the sea of waves
That crash upon my sights.
Beware for I am a bullet en route to the enemy.
Be a bullet with me tonight.
I am bound to leave.
I have found no reason to chase you
For you are indeed a dream I will forget
As soon as sunrise takes over moonlight's devise.
Sped fast into darkness searching for clarity's light,
In the face of the unknown.

I Can Be Good; I Can Be Gone

I can be good; I can be gone.
In a lucid dream you and I
Shook the world completely.
Take arms for when they come
This way with filed teeth
And poison-dipped claws.
I can be good; I can be gone.
In a drunken blur
You and I were gods.
Yeah, we fought all night.
All I remember is the scream of silver bullets
Like flying dragons down Broadway.
I can be good; I can be gone.
And here I go.

Subliminal

My, what wonderful webs you've woven.
What magical strands you construct.
You were made to unify.
You were designed to lead us.
Won't you weave a life for me to live free?
Won't you let me paint a masterpiece?
Put me in the background;
Make me subliminal.

Who Sent You?

I've gone overboard on this one,
Letting my heart take the helm and run with it,
And now I'm headed to you,
Letting my heart take the wheel,
But knowing that I'm headed for you
Makes all the difference.
Knowing I'm headed for you
Keeps the fire going,
And I will rage against the storm
That never dies and create my own.

I Was Here and Once Mattered

I've found a fortune
Beyond measure in you.
I've found bandages
And wrappings in your words,
In your every breath.
This will keep me alive,
Long enough to fight the tide
That's coming.
Long enough to stab the earth
With my flag and say, "I was here,
And I once mattered."

Below the Line

I wish there was an easier way,
But I must cross this bridge alone.
I wish there was a way to beat this ugly notion.
I'm swimming in the ocean, loving the motion around me.
Lately I'm in love but she doesn't know.
She can't know or I'll burn another bridge
And fall below the line of stable.
I'm always just trying to get home before midnight.

Hardly

I'm on the road to a place of serenity.
I'm taking this trip to get away,
But the farther I go
The more I regret it.
I miss your jungle eyes;
That glow keeps me alive.
She said "The only opinion that matters
Is your own, and mine; it should mean something by now."
I'd like to play a game with you when I get back.
And until I get back, keep glowing on;
You hardly ever leave my thoughts.

Freight Train

Their eyes pass over me, without knowing my tale.
It's cool though, I don't mind, and I keep them out of mine.
I try to hold onto the power beneath my skin.
I am a freight train underneath this sleep-deprived face.
I am on my way to perfection, and then some.

I Could Say a Thing or Two

I could say a thing or two
'Bout what I am to you,
Just a face in a long list
Of not good enough,
Just a friend you don't love that much.
I could say a thing or two
About where I fit in with the truth
Of this lonely heart and what it's been through,
But I bet you'd never believe it.

A.I.W.I.L.

I've given so much of myself
Lately for nothing in return.
I didn't ask to walk the path a ghost.
I didn't ask but now I'm concerned.
You give so much of yourself away,
But never to me.
You push away my energy like it could be
The death of you, baby.
All I want is...
Well, I think I've said this already.

Middle of the Road

Time tore me to pieces
Just to see if I could heal.
Just to see if I could come
Back from the point of breaking.
I have mended my wounds;
They've become beautiful scars on my heart.
There is energy there, a roaring fire.
I've always loved
Random moments
Far away from a plan,
Far away from the norm.
Middle of the road
And nowhere to go.

Stay Awake Soul

I woke up today thinking,
"Stay awake soul,
Survive a little longer,
But don't drag it out.
Know when it's your turn to go
And leave things for dead.
Know when to cut the line.
Know when you're out of your head.
Know when to ask for help,
Or experience hell again."

A Season for Collisions

Win some, lose some, try the best
You can, to walk away with your head
Held high at the end of sixty minutes.
This is a season for collisions, with
Long bombs toward the end zone.
Check yourself at the door,
Before you wrap yourself up in armour,
And face the opposition like a pride of lions.

Temptress

I see the ceiling lifting up
Revealing a temptress
Smoking a purple cigarette,
Black lipstick
And a white skull covering her smile.
I wonder what secrets she keeps under lock and key.
I wonder if maybe I'm one of them secretly.

You Can Always Try

I love how you listen, tag along,
And don't ask any questions.
Maybe I'm mad still,
Going off like this again.
Maybe my ride has flown without me.
So, I'll hitchhike through this world instead,
Because more of my heart is gone now,
Buried in the ground.
More of me wants to be found.
Every time I watch you leave,
I go further into the forest of my mind.
Little by little I separate;
At this rate, there won't be anything left
For you to love,
But you can try.
You can always try.

Under Ground, You Say

He whispered to himself,
As he rocked back and forth,
"I keep hating myself a little more
Tonight, why can't I conquer
This terrible habit?
I used to be more, when I didn't
Give myself away for free, for the sake
Of conversation.
Here you are, hearts just ripped out,
Things still beating and warm.
Oh, all the scars I carry inside my skull.
All the faces, buried in the ground,
And scattered in the sea."

Goodnight, Sweet Delusion

Continue to make a stand
In the snow, dress well, dress warm
'Cause January siphons
Years and strength right off the bones,
Another stranger lost in his own land.
Why here, of all places?
I say this like I can't move on,
Like this city of bridges hasn't put a spell
On me, and I can't drive away,
But I purified my heart.
And next up, I'm changing
My levels, waiting for the storm
To run its course,
Annihilate your anger; leave it there in the earth.
Leave it at the source, for this river made of used pages
Lays scattered, under a full moon,
Under a star-filled sky,
Goodnight sweet delusion.

Own Up

Just because you saw yourself in her eyes,
Doesn't mean it was going to work out.
It's your fault you got attached.

Soaking Up the Mood

I realize now, you weren't my life;
You were only a sentence,
In a brief chapter.
You were just a side character making
A cameo appearance.
I'm done with your double face.
You left me to rot while
I was out of my mind chasing
The moon's reflection.
I found life after you
And it was easier to do
Than I thought.
Silence two steps
Round the room now,
Soaking up the mood.

Ameliorate

Gimme the time of day,
And I'll fill up a page
In front of your face.
Gimme a minute to take these
Imperfections and I'll turn them to gold.
I'll take broken souls
And give them a reason to sing.

Sorry, I Don't Love Your Art

He lifted a book in his hand,
As he rummaged through the garbage
On the conveyer belt,
And said, "See, bestseller,"
Implying I wasn't there yet.
I wanna prove him wrong so
I keep praying,
"Pretty, pretty, please Jesus,
Maybe someday?"
And then I'm reminded that
Even a bestseller can find
Itself in the garbage pile.
So, who cares?
I'll leave my story here when I'm gone,
For faces to flip through my pages,
Ima keep writing regardless, thanks.
I'm climbing a mountain by trusting you,
Don't lemme down, okay?

On the Shelf

Though I am unknown,
I'm right beside you on the shelf.
At least the greats can
Play music for you, forever.
One day I'll join you into that forever,
Into that unknown realm.
A life without you, a world without you, is lonely.
Still, I press on, as I have always done.
Slapping down fractured emotions in a moment
And wishing I could have lived alternative ones.
I'll leave behind these parts of me,
And when you reach the end
Of my ink, you will be different.
I'm right up there beside you guys on the shelf.
And while nobody knows or cares about my name,
I'm still up there with you.

Scattered on the Road

They tried siphoning my love
For you, so I'd be empty.

I fought off the fury
And unleashed my own.

I held myself together
When I wanted to be scattered
On the road like someone's car crash.

Dear Hope

I thought I could find love
On my own, but I was wrong to think something
Beautiful might happen without your approval.
Father above, be merciful;
Help me to understand
Who I am in all this chaos,
'Cause lately stepping outside
Feels like I'm walking
Through an endless valley of graves.
So I stay up late at night, unleashing my mind,
Hoping to be a lighthouse
Because the world will try
To drown you in its many storms repeatedly till
You drift to the bottom.
I've lived as a star on its way out,
About to go supernova.
Dear hope,
I'm leaving a bread crumb trail
Behind so others will know where
This passion started.
So they can follow my struggle and
Know you're not unattainable.

Fortress

Last night was full of psychedelic visions,
Illuminating sights as I travelled
Through the spirit realm, no longer
Nothing to my name, supernatural moments
Where I felt one with God's love and blessing,
No longer wasted potential.
My breath was visible in the frozen air,
And you tell me it's not real?
Where did this fictional delusion come from then?
Imagination ablaze like fireworks in October sky
Reanimate my heart, make it into a fortress
That nothing can sabotage.

Don't Be So Happy, Please

Seems like lately,
Everything I make
Bares blood-soaked fangs.

Every time I think I've
Found her, she leaves.

And every time I try to smile
Someone cuts me off from the reason for it.

How do I solve this ongoing equation?

You act like
You don't know the answer,
Just to humour me.

Grand Risings

She started saying
Grand risings, recently,
So I joined her cause of retiring
Good morning for good.
With caffeine in my veins,
I'm ready to face the day,
And all its many ways.
So live like today is the end of one state
Of being and the continuation of the spirit self.
Leave your burdens
And push on dead ahead.
And late at night,
Every time the moon
Shines, every time you close
Your eyes, you're standing right there,
In front of me saying, "This photo is old,
And I'm not into it anymore."

Intercepted

I'm trying to pause,
Breathe in breathe out, focus.
There is more to this picture perfect
Winter wonderland, than what's going on inside my head.
Oh so much chaos, can't stay though,
Gotta show you something more.
I could be a temple
For you to find your centre,
And you could stay there,
Though you throw me off balance.
You sink my ships of hope with cannon balls
Shot outta your mouth.
You intercepted my message in a bottle.
That was the last one I ever finished.

That's a Bit Over Dramatic, Don't You Think?

He held his chest, looked up at the sky and said,
"I don't have one anymore...
You stole it when you left
Earth without saying goodbye...
I mean, I still have the urge
To call a number that won't pick up anymore.
So, I immerse myself in a world of words
To pass the time, keeping my mind
Sharp by filling up notebooks.
I'm not that animated
Cartoon character anymore.
That part of me died
With my twenties.
What a waste, what a blur,
I hardly remember the faces
That surrounded me on those weekends.
That so-called tight group of friends
And acquaintances.
We grew apart and
I don't feel a thing for the
Ones who abandoned me.
I kicked them out of
My heart so many years ago.
Now I'm kicking myself for
Dusting off this memory I no longer need.

I Say It One Time, Then I Say It No Mo

I breathe liquid nitrogen vapours when
My back is against a wall.
I speak ice when I feel another's rage.
I know there is more to this nightmare,
And what I stand for won't vanish like the hours.
All these ghosts speak to me tonight,
All these sirens sing "come join the rocks
And the sea."
But I can't reply.
Morality, on board a ghost ship,
In a second, in a post card, in a letter in a bottle,
Everything can morph.

Half

You were with me through the dorm room escapades.
I remember the night some sales types
Stacked garbage cans outside my dorm entrance
Hoping to get the best of me in the morning,
But I wasn't there.
I was in your bed, late night romance instead
Of memorizing pitches.
They were jealous of our flames.
We weren't allowed to love each other;
We did anyways.
At least one of us did.
I thought I'd found my other half,
But you weren't even half of what I needed you to be.

Tatiana

How much of myself
Will I lose tonight by letting
You into my life?
How many cities
Will you abandon
Before you call one home?
You're alone in this silent
Black and white movie.
You edited me out,
Didn't want my love,
Didn't care for my words,
When they were an extension of my soul.
Maybe it's destiny calling us
To separate and head to opposite ends
Of the earth?
It could be; I think it is.

Colours

I change colours when I feel like it.
I need to step back from the mantle.
I'm through here, I think my days with you
Are over like a dream of seconds being crushed.
Colours in my dreams,
Except for the night you lied.
Saying everything was black and white.
I remember seeing
Yours leave your eyes first,
Then the rest followed,
Myself closely behind.

If Only I Could Pick the Colours

Colour the canvas red like her hair.
Fill in her eyes blue and sometimes in August, green.
Paint her lips black.
Her teeth white.
Her aura gold.
I'm just a rough sketch compared to her.
If only I could pick the colours.

If Only 1965

If only 1965, Venice Beach, me
And the revolving doors, syncing minds.

Saying, "How many can we open?"

I would've loved to meet you, man.
We could've compared our mad language.

If only 1985 had given me
The same stars in my eyes
Yours had.

What Happened in the Desert?

A shaman told them to open the doors,
To see what there was to see beyond vision.
They consumed the plant
And danced in the desert
Speaking of giant snakes slithering.
These reflections of car crashes
In nowhere land.
This obsession with the end,
Was only just the beginning of legend.

Worth My While

Ruby roses in your golden hair,
The seduction of your body
Ties me to the bed as I stare into
Your moon eyes wondering
About these wolves
Calling your name in the dark tonight.
Will they tear you to pieces,
Or guide you farther home?
Blow out the candles
In silence, make it worth my while.

Hands of Fate,

Oh, hands of fate,
Reverberate from the wall.
I hear every sound that isn't you.
Don't you have to leave now, your
Carriage awaits, and it's almost midnight.
I haven't a clue what to call you,
Or where to go in the winter,
Somewhere with sun and sand.
Once I had you in my sights,
I knew you'd haunt my life
If I didn't say hello.

Almost Worshipped

You were once my obsession,
But I will not wait in line while you
Flirt with the world.
You're not mine, and that's fine
By me; I've changed my taste
And my intentions with you,
Now over.
But there was a time
When I almost worshipped you.

It's Been a Minute

Glass and porcelain,
Icicles and snowflakes,
Newborn puppies and kittens,
Promises of love.
First dates,
Vows and weddings,
Soulmates ice skating, so very slowly,
Just barely moving,
But thankful for their moments
Of movement.
This place is only a
Temporary home,
While I wait for the kingdom
To pop up like a painting.
She said, "You shelter a beautiful perspective,
And spice your sentences with straight up emotion,
And a loyalty like no other.
It's been a minute,
And an honour to know you."

Weathered Still Frame

You splattered black paint onto blank canvas,
And created a story of a moment long past,
About an era forgotten when animals
Pulled wagons and men only lived a blink of an eye,
Dying from loneliness, too much booze and tuberculosis.
You achieved your tale found in visuals like a magician on stage.
And the result left me speechless, like being woken up by an angel.

Walks by the River

Today I'm cutting off all strings.
The hold you had on me
Was hell because I couldn't be set free from
The darkness that crawled outta your mouth,
After I said it wasn't mutual.
I learned to ignore you and
Cross that bridge on my own,
To reclaim my life
From the skeletal hands of winter.
It's summer right now,
So take walks while I
Watch you leave my life,
Like a passing river.

Your Last Sentences Always Get Me in the Feels

By the way you're glowing, I can see you're honestly smitten.
But I am best alone, locked in a room writing for hours,
Walking away with something more then I had before.
The moment froze, for just a second, a slight hesitation,
A heavy exhale as the demons from below tug and pull at my ankles.
Whispering, "Remember your dark vision?
You survived a war from within;
God and the angels must love you to pieces."

Chicken Seasoning

Mr. Trainer Man walks up
To say, "Sorry young man,
There's just not enough seasoning.
I want some chicken
With my seasoning
If you know what I mean.
Just not enough herbs
On this fallen bird.
Give it a second breath,
Give it some more, always more,
And stop the unnecessary walking."

He Must've Guided You

He must've guided you,
He must've opened your heart
And told you to leave the nest.
You crossed oceans
With no sense of doubt;
You trusted in his good nature
To see you through.
He must've guided you,
He must've brought you to me.

Be There

I want to love today,
Despite still being a stranger to it.
I want to enjoy these hours that slide by without fail,
Before white bleaches all the colour yesterday once held.
I want to be there for you,
When you forget what it used to look like.

The Vault

You are a vault of unfulfilled promises.
You said those words and shook my hand
Knowing you wouldn't pay me back,
Knowing you wouldn't keep your word,
Like someone I used to call brother.
You will always be a vault of darkness,
And you are twisted beyond belief,
And I'm not saying I'm a saint either,
But I put all my time into this,
While you don't even
Use your heart anymore.
What froze it over?
What do I do with the memories of us
Drinking black
Coffee late into the night?
We wrote poems late into
The night, and called it quits
After putting together something
In the spirit of the beat generation.
Maybe one day, we will
Reconnect our dots,
And we can look beyond the debt
You owe me and they can read it too.
Until then, it stays in the vault.

Is It Night?

Stepping out of my shadow,
Looking up at the light in the sky,
I often wonder about my own,
And if I have a purpose, is it nigh?
Did you put this desire in me?
This fire for words, that never runs empty.
As days slide past, my pens bleed
Honesty and I can't seem to stop it.

At the Pier

At the pier, she looked back,
She was going on into the future without him.
Both their hearts were wounded,
But they would repair one day.
They would survive, though the pain
Was unbearable.
They'd both been broken before,
And they would heal again.
She whispered to herself,
"All roads are lonely,
Especially the one going home,
So I will try the sea."
And her in tatters, and him in ribbons.
She looked back at him in tears.
Never again would she seek the love of a ghost.
Never again would he be so quick to trust a pretty face.

Forecast

Her gaze was fixated on the path ahead,
With long black hair and emerald eyes that
Burned through windowpanes on this train
Ride from France to Spain.
She longed to return home among the angels,
And missed her heart dearly, who was a doctor.
He loved her fiercely; soon they would reunite.
The forecast tonight would be fireworks,
And red wine to blot out the lonely world's sighs.

Ditch the Drama

Ditch the drama,
Leave it at the door;
You only harm yourself
Breathing life back into what broke you.
You only cut yourself off from Heaven.
One day you will see that this planet
Is a dying horse, and people still wanna ride it.
You can give it all the food and water you want,
But it's dying and it may not survive
The winter like this.

Dead Skin

You kept me standing when I wanted
To lay down and die.
You watched me losing my mind, twice.
I can't go back
To those sliding doors
With no locks,
The blue clothing,
And the meal trays with my name on them,
Trusting no one in my own confusion,
Deeply delusional.
Well, I'm saying no,
I won't break down again.
I am a poet before I am on the clock,
I can't leave my body just yet;
I've got books to write, and webs to spin
Late into January nights.
All colourful language aside,
Summer is what I'm after.
I'm looking forward
To swimming in the river,
Bike rides, BBQ's,
Sitting in a canoe,
Fishing, thunderstorms,
And that feeling of purity in the air

When it rains.
I wonder who I will meet this year,
And who I will lose.
Friends move away and disconnect
All the time, so
It's fine if I never meant a thing
To you, go ahead and leave me
Behind without a sound.
You showed me your truth,
And I shed you like dead skin.
Black out? No.
I still have lights in my life.

Chaos at First Sight

I know we've only just met,
But we could set this city on fire,
If you're up for it.
All the while laughing,
All the while two-stepping
Through depression once again,
While we sing the anthem of a burning world.

Best Life

A loud noise rips me out of a beautiful dream,
Reality screaming at me at the top of its lungs.
Out of a great northern blue, I still have faith in
Your truth, and no matter what I may face,
You are there to calm the waves
And make it safe.
My best life whispers, "Unleash us, soldier.
Dear light, you asked for this.
Remember you asked for this,
Don't forget your promise."

Skydiving

Then he felt it,
Thorns piercing the skin
And the smell wasn't enough
To outweigh the searing pain in his veins.

"You hurt, don't you dear,"
She said with a smile.

No, it's only discomfort.

Losing you feels amazing,
Like skydiving to freedom.

Timeless Echo

In your room of colour and design,
In your daydreams you find the will
To leap from reality into the arms of imagination.
Hold close now, don't ever let go,
For there is safety in these bright lights from your mind;
There is purpose that burns like a violet star in the sky;
There is possibility roaming free,
In March's inevitable departure from frozen prairie nights.
In this timeless echo dwells veteran underground artists,
Feeding the monster within, that's never really satisfied.

Under a Roof of Chatter

I stepped inside a dead beehive,
But at least it's not an active hornet's nest.
At least I can unleash my best,
But you won't be able to read it.
I stand under a roof of chatter,
And listen to the rain inside my head.
I am a vault of darkness without you in my life.

The Busted-Up Wolves

Yesterday's news still rings in my eardrums,
Having ripped off the bolts of my heart's doors something
fierce.
They slammed shut,
To give you privacy for the sudden mourning you must do.
This monster stole life from you before;
I still remember the wound.
My temple collapses in silence to let you adjust, but not alone.
You're one of my brothers, and the busted-up
Wolves in my heart howl beside yours.

So Many Words

First, I wrote you a letter, titled "Keep on breathing."
When you didn't respond I was crushed.
When you said nothing,
I died a little more when you kept my last letter.
You finally wrote back saying it was used to start a fire.
I thought the fact that you were angelic,
That you would use your heart
Like a long-ago sailor using the stars at sea.
I thought maybe your direction
Would lead back to me, just like it used to.
You used to be so many things to me,
I used to feel such electricity.
So many words from your mouth,
But "I love you" was never one of them.

Someone Else

As you listed what the catch
To your beauty was,
I realized we weren't compatible.
I couldn't see the two
Of us becoming electric;
The chemistry wasn't there.
I couldn't imagine growing old with you.
But maybe someone else will.

Drops

Along the way,
I forgave you.
I waited for heavenly signs
To wake me from
This dream
That feels like
Too much absinthe.
I'm still waiting
And I haven't touched
A drop in years.

Names I'll Never Get to Call You

Go on and burn beautifully, blue flame.
I'm awake, I see you tonight, starry-eyed
And watching you blaze ever so brightly.
I see you now, so go on and show the world
Who you're really meant to be, extraordinary soul.
Your story is inspiring to someone holding on by a fishing line
Of hope, lost like me.
I only recently realized; you've been guiding me all this time.
And though I have all these names I'll never get to call you,
You still retain full access to my weathered heart.
It still remembers you in January.

The Glasses Do Nussing

I dove down to bring her proof
There were others before us.
I swam up from the ocean's grasp,
Clutched in my hands, Egyptian gold.
We coasted for months
Surviving insanity alone with lust.
It's strong and greater still
Than our climax spent
Dreaming that we could hold on
To the ropes just a little longer.
That we could survive our demons
And all the violence beneath us.
I am blind to it, just as you're blind to me.
You don't see me anymore,
You just see my strings.

Strawberries on the Road

I wonder if they ever noticed
They lost some of their groceries.
They were in such a rush to go,
They left all these strawberries on the road.
And every passing car paints them
Like exploding stars upon my shoulders.

Raspberries and Tequila

She tasted like raspberries and tequila.
She walked in and out with me on her arm.
She knew what she wanted, a distraction,
An excuse not to leave the bed.
We spent the night under the stars
Watching them twinkle and glow.
She was sweeter than anything I'd ever had,
Dressed in pink and diamonds,
On a mission to feed her wolves.

Delonix Magia

In a garden such as this, we exist.
Our branches provide shade and reach out.
Our ruby leaves shimmer in the sunlight.
And you could climb us, if you wanted,
But that's not for everyone.
And you could carve your name,
If you thought it would leave a legacy,
But caution, we bleed flames...

Tossed Flowers Over a Grave Idea

These days, I'm hunting for a new bombshell.

I may have already found her,
So I left with a smile.

I find the pieces
Show themselves more now
That I know what I'm looking for.

And I will follow my nose into this soap shop,
'Cause I bet it smells amazing.

The woman at the counter

Commands the lineup.
I bet she tastes
Even better
Than chocolate
Caramel ice cream.

I love the feeling of new sounds so
I still shop for music.

I need to feed
This creature,

So I leave a million
Poems in my wake.

And I love too much.
It always causes
My heart to shatter,
But these days it's a phoenix..

It always takes a little more away,
That's the catch.

You are not the first
To ruin something special and beautiful,
And you won't be the last.

All that's left are these
Tossed flowers
Over a grave idea.

I keep haunting this city,
Hoping one day my nightmare
Will become someone's heavenly dream.

A Dozen Roses

I almost bought a dozen roses for you today.
I thought about it, but I'm gonna wait.
Not because you're not worth it.
You are, I just don't wanna be too over the top so soon.
I don't wanna scare you away
With this hopeless, romantic heart.

Venus Fly Trap

Remove the spiritual cancers from me,
As I press on through this year's hardships,
And let me be like a Venus fly trap;
Let evil be the fly.

Holy Tree

I spark you up and move around the room,
Instantly soothing me.
Take me for another journey
Around the sun, please.
Take me to your holy branches
Hanging over the years to come.
I wanna stay clear with a razor mind,
And purge myself of venom.

Orchards

The venom that dwells in me wants out,
But I can no longer be its vessel as time chips away.
Morality raises its quiet voice, and I can no longer ignore it.
I hear your calm voice through the realms,
Reminding me that I was born separate from darkness.
That tar figure of evil reaches out trying to rip my heart
From my chest like someone picking an apple from a tree.
There is a barrier, a force of unseen power that keeps me
Deeply rooted to the orchards of life.

Birch Tree

Carve your name into a birch tree with me,
'Cause the butterflies love to hover over yonder.
They come with May and come what may,
I may choose to stay and watch the metamorphosis take over.
Wild colours spill over my life's pages but that's okay,
I never wanted them to be blank anyways.
I invite all this and more.
I'm ready to carve my earth name beside yours.

The Woodlands

I thought about the woodlands,
Living in your eyes, and all the birds
And animals that had homes in them.
I thought about starting a fire there
Between us, so we'd both blaze
Underneath the stars.

Into October

Into October I march.
I press on into the cold.
The valley is golden,
And all the green is gone.
It's all gone.
"It's time to die now," the trees say.
"It's time to die, but not for good.
We will return the same as before
And completely new, soon.
And we will still remember you,
Who walks and loves and breathes underneath our shade.
Who kisses fair maidens goodnight and drinks until
A new day replaces the hours.
You, who spills passion out of a pen's ink.
Who lives for the now but does not forget the past.
We will remember being a chapter in your tale just as you
Will be in ours."

Aging With the Trees

I grow older with every setting sun;
I can feel it in my bones, in my muscles.
I can hear it in my voice,
Age finally creeping up on me,
And here I thought I would stay
Twenty for always.
If I can be a sharper blade
Than I was yesterday,
Maybe that's all I need.
See, I'm just aging with the trees,
Losing leaves along the way.

Who I Am

I'm wishing, praying, hoping
For a clear exit from the current way I pay my bills.
I want to bloom, to fully understand who I am in all this chaos.
But that's easy to do when I know I am a poem.

Anhedonia

I could go out,
Have a night on the town,
And still feel no satisfaction
On what used to ail my winter blues.
These thoughts of you, how could I forget?
You're like the only reason to stay,
But I'm not looking to jet, just yet.
I'll let this feeling baptize me like a wave.
I went out on the town tonight,
And almost felt something.

In Passing

Her eyes are like lilacs, like
Campfires crackling in the night.
Her ways are always with the best of intentions,
They always feel right.
Like shooting stars, like the glow of the moon.
Like gold among the common stones.
She always wears a strong perfume like roses in June.
I wonder if she's ever valued me the
Same way I do in passing.

At the Theatre

And with that, the play came
Screeching to a halt,
Lights turned back on and
The curtains closed.
The show was over, but something had changed.
It was only until he looked
In the mirror that he noticed
The gun shot wound in his tuxedo...

Sorry

Bright candy colours on the walls
Remind me of her neon mind, and how
She could always provide light when I went dark.
I think back to that last time I saw her when she
Asked me for my heart, that look she gave me when I
Said "Sorry, it's already taken."
It ripped her apart like a pride of lions attacking an old gazelle.

Gore

We sat in our seats at the rodeo,
As the bulls tried to
Throw off their riders.
Those wild beasts tried
To gore and trample them to death.
But the cowboys escaped without damage.

Gun Slinger

She's like, "My ways
Are perfect, flawless and
Beautiful in any light
And they hypnotize unaware
Minds waiting at the finish line.
And you wanna give up and go back,
But you just made a promise.
So focus on the path ahead of
These neglected roads and abandoned vehicles.
Have you conquered your demons yet?
Or is it still same old same old heart attack
Hold on your soul?
Quit saying 'I don't think
I can bear living my life without you,
I'm in it till the end, sapphire.'
And I'm always cold dead centre, 'cause
January knows me oh so well by now;
It never leaves me.
I sent that ghost back to hell with spiritual bullets.
And I'll send yours back as well."

Walk Away

Even though I've already destroyed
You in my head, in my heart
The pen says otherwise.
It whispers "More."
You're no different then the many strangers
Passing by me around the city.
Faces I'll never get to know,
Going places I'll never need to travel.
So it is also with you, that this last nail
Is hammered into your memory.
And I'll walk away as you bleed out.

When the Night Comes

When the night comes,
And you are living on the edge,
Painting the town red,
Head spinning, remember to stay grounded.
And no matter what is said,
Know every single second is a gift
From the One who bled and died
For your sins.
When the night comes again,
Like a pack of Utahraptors,
Remember His words can
Save your tormented soul
From the sickle claws of evil.

Temporarily Disconnected

This was the soundtrack of my madness,
When I was temporarily disconnected
From the real, chasing ghosts
And having conversations with strangers.
I didn't care, I just needed
To feel like I was still human,
Relating one on one, to stay a person
Not a lost cause.
They all gave up on me, but you;
You stayed by my side until hell
Fell back into the earth.

Benefit of the Doubt

I let protected words outta my mouth,
Giving you the benefit of the doubt
That you'll keep 'em to yourself.
I got a long way to go before I don't need any help.
Digging in deep, becoming something else.
A red and white starlight sky whispers,
"Have you ever felt the weight of language
Bring a building down?"

Party

At the party, everyone was
Smiling, laughing, feasting.
I spoke with many as
Hours were devoured
In the presence
Of family and friends.
We started a fire and told
Stories you wouldn't believe,
Still lingering in mad night,
As the engine of my mind spewed noise.
And I kept coming back to you,
Back to me, back to us
Before the war.
I kept coming to us, thinking,
Will I ever be this alive
In the flesh again?
Capturing moments,
And even as I madly jot this down...
No!
Come back seconds!
You were there,
And then you ghosted us.

Cheater

I woke to see you already gone,
A note by my phone; you went ahead
Without me, so long.
You've never been mine, but now
I see it's impossible to find solace.
You didn't say you were spoken for,
Somehow forgetting to mention that
This could never last,
To never enjoy the moments
With you by my side again;
And all the while, the games you played,
Cheating with every single hand.

Encore

I've been planning a dream to
Speak back to me like a conversation
Among best friends.
I put my all into ink, watching
While it piles up and covers my image.
My words live in boxes and bookshelves,
And regardless of where I go, it politely knocks
On my door saying, "Please, just one more poem."
One more percentage of my life forever
Mummified in these pages.
I can hear the buzz, the encore.

Love Letters

I'm keeping all your love letters
And storing them together for later tonight
When I'll use them to feed the firepit.
I'll shed whatever remains of my river of sorrows
And look up to the sky.
That's where you're going, into the atmosphere
Just like the pollution you caused in my life.

Leaving with the Last Word

I wade through the ocean
Of oil and garbage your foul mouth spat out,
Just trying to say goodbye.
All that pollution
Just for the sake of leaving
With the last word.

Hunter (of Hearts)

You drown me in a dark
And stormy ocean of sound,
Emotions translated into music.
God bless these artists,
Bleeding poetry from their souls,
Flowing audio magma captured by microphones.
The sound of seduction is destructive,
Because she loves the thrill and challenge
Of owning the hearts of every single guy
In the room by midnight. Go,
Return to your family of sirens.
I swear you'll return to them empty handed.

Dang

Blonde maiden,
How many hearts do you have in jars of formaldehyde?
How many trophies of those
Who got lost in the woodlands of
Your eyes and world?

For Sport

I reflect on the day I met you,
So random and surreal.
Because God made you so beautiful,
You stole my heart without even trying.
And you tried it on, but threw it away
Once you had it,
As if it was for sport.

I Devour the Hours

I devour the hours like a hungry great white shark,
Feasting on an injured diver in a bloody frenzy.
I am a ravenous tiger tearing up a foolish local.
I am blood and stones; I am armour and swords clashing
Like a modern knight raging against an ancient army.
I am ashes and bones lost at sea.
I am over you, lost love.
I pace back and forth for the fourth time this month.
I am jungles and wild birds and creatures who holler
Out the maker's infinite glory.
I came through snow and ice to live this life and when
I return to the earth, I will no longer ache or hurt
For you, old friend that lives in the palace of my heart.
You're that guiding star I follow on walks alone.
I look up at the sky at midnight saying a prayer,
Hoping you're listening when I am blue and lonely.
I am still solo in this wilderness.
Stay on guard for it will try to chew you up
And vomit you out for sport.
I go off into the star-filled night and sing songs
No one else will hear but God.
I'll sing them for you, if you'd bother listening
All the way through
The silence of fortresses and kingdoms

I do not know the names of.
I am a cemetery of quiet thoughts,
Haunting the sea and all those broken
Down sailors who miss land, their seemingly
Never ending pursuit of gold, silver
And jewels from kings that didn't make the journey home.
They died out there, searching for glory,
Searching for God and finding only wise men
Who thought they were gods,
But who were humbled with age.
All their stories never passing on,
All their potential will die with
This letter in a bottle.
Like web from a spider,
I weave my soul through pen and microphone
In hopes it will save someone else in the process,
As I devour the hours and fade with night.

A Falling Leaf

If writing books is endless, then
I wish to write to you for eternity, Lord.
Please don't leave me alone,
For without you I am a falling leaf,
Awaiting the death of its season.

Cemetery Season

I'm on day six of a long line of days
To go before I can say I've quit smoking.
So far so good; I am restless as a puppy
Excited about playing fetch.
I'm full of hopes in a winter romance;
If such a thing happens, I'll be ready.
I am a castaway on a great titanic ship,
Sailing down the Atlantic taking in the sights of
Dancing whales and seagulls causing movement in the sky.
Old sky above me, timeless sky above me,
God above me, let me be like an eagle catching salmon.
Let me love like an elephant, always remembering those
That turned to bones in this cemetery season, silent
And still like my heart the moment she left my life.

Ever Stop to Think?

Ever stop to think
How things could've been
Had she not died at twenty?

Would she have a ring
On her finger at twenty-three?

And kids by twenty-six?

Would her husband
Spoil her every chance he got?

I know I would've.
She would've been worth it.

Industrial Sounds

Industrial sounds clang
And echo in the hallways of my soul,
Like saw blades carving wooden sculptures,
And hammers hitting nails.
I wonder how my rusty self-esteem
Will survive the rainfall that goes on
Behind my eyes, because I never let 'em out.
How many tear drops will spill
Out of my good intentions?
Rejected like the last desperate dame
Who wanted me when there was zero chemistry.
I didn't mean to shatter her fragile heart to pieces,
But I had to be honest,
'Cause we were fire and dry forest,
And I am the blue flame
That turns everything to ashes.
I'm not giving you the time of day,
Or time to breathe because
Old, Jack Frost is nigh,
En route to a city near you, citizen.
When he gets here, I will change into ice,
So mind your feet.
We are circuses and asylums,
And we could be a part of it and never know,
And never grow as individuals
With any worth to our names.

Singing Songs from Portugal

Oh, I played the notes,
From out of the blue,
From out of the dark night sky.
I sang three songs
Hoping she was nigh.
She was a no show,
So I kept on writing
Tales of salvation
About you, and me,
And every soul who ever believed in God.
I sang a song for all of us
Beneath the stars that night.
A song of love and longing
And wished you were the one
To light my way in life.

The Wanderer

He sat by the stream,
A secret place to unwind,
Where the sun is in full display and
Energy is kind to lonely wanderers.
He strummed his guitar and sang his songs.
May all the days of your life
Be full of love and music only you can make.

N

You spit raw energy on a microphone,
Slaying the competition.
Of all the ways to stay in my head
You placed yourself in songs and I feel
Them bumpin' through my veins.
You write pieces with a clean mouth.
I know what that's about, hero;
Write bangers for infinity, please.

Jaded Lullaby

The night sings her sweet
Jaded lullaby, so I move to it.
I want more while I have vinegar in my bones,
Air in these lungs and purpose for my presence.
This machine I control only ever
Wanted to be yours to hold.

Metal Head

Head banging and writing to metal,
As waves overcome my senses.
It feeds the beasts within,
Satisfies their thirst and hunger.
They're blood drunk and addicted.
Spin the cd's and fall in love with the sound.

Tired

I found a way, found a way, far from you.
It's okay, it's okay, you want the truth?
I'm lonely, kind of distant, turning blue.
I found your name, found your name,
It set me loose.
This new love will not do, it will not do.
Please remove your heart before
It starts a fire soon.
Desire will only end one way; I hate it too.
I'm just so tired of watching the world
With a noose around its throat,
So tired of watching it go up in flames.

Fall of My Rome

I feel like I am less than I was, before.
I feel like I am less than I was, before.
I feel like I am less than I was, before,
The fall of my Rome,
Fall of my Rome.

Battle Myself Again

I need to battle myself again, self again, let go.
I've gotta battle myself again, self again, in the nighttime glow.
I've gotta win this war my friend, war my friend, will I make it home?
I'm tryin' to battle myself again, self again, in all this snow.

I Decided

I decided long ago,
That I'd never even listen,
And I'll try and fail for you.

I decided so long ago,
That I'd never see this rerun,
And I'll hold the line for truth.

I once decided very long ago
That I'd never get over your beauty
Even if the memory tears me in two.

Blue Violin

Blue violin
You sing in the night,
You cry when the light
Comes to call
'Cause you're most alive
When the moon fills
Earth with promises of love lines.
I hear your song as I write.
Blue violin
How you fill my ears
With a blissful sound,
Like a sound so full of life.
Blue violin, you can make
An entire crowd bawl their eyes out
Without even trying.

The Faintest of Sounds Goes a Long Way

It's a classic sound
I've been saving for a night
Like this one; oh what fun
We could have chasing shadows with torches,
Killing the dark that's deep within us.
Beyond flesh and blood
Lays the starlight of your soul.
We are beyond broken records,
Playing the same song, always the same
Song and never growing tired of it.
I knew when I first saw you, you'd be
A lifeline, adorned in gold and diamonds,
With a smile on your face
That demands attention, babe.
Oh, what a wonderfully random day,
The faintest of sounds goes a long way.

Midnight's Choir

Let's try to pretend
That you and I aren't a sad story.
But the monuments you built
To fill the void have collapsed,
And the wreckage buried
Your good intentions with broken
Stones, the bones of your youth, imploded.
Now only memories of smiles
And laughter that died with midnight's
Choir, once again, a wound medicine could not heal.

Finger Snaps

The music washes over my senses,
Waves of bass pass through me
Like the Holy Ghost.
In an instant I'm transported without taking
A step or making a move.
Just like that, finger snaps and I'm leaving Earth
Looking back with a smile.

Free Fall

I am like fresh snow: silent, weightless.
I've been in free fall since you left me,
Still waiting to hit the ground.

Save One

Down by the gentle stream,
I sat to wash my dreams clean,
Make them beautiful pieces of art.
And for all my efforts they were restored,
Almost all of them, save one.
There's no way to resurrect the dead
With these weathered hands.

Fear

She said, "Yesterday It wasn't raining, but the water works
were on, Hun, they were pouring outta me, and I was stunned.
Today, my faith in humanity is drowning in the river.
You'd think it would come up for air,
But it just sits there sinking deeper into the next realm,
Watching oxygen leave its lungs.
I searched for happiness once, but you left me in silence
At the bottom of my world,
Face to face with my fear.
But I was the one who walked away with hands dripping red."

Here in Spirit

You still check in
From time to time in winter.

I feel you here in spirit,
But you're too afraid to use
Your voice.

So you use your other one,
The one that makes no sound.

Congratulations Sir, You've Just Won a Ghost!

I could've gone back for you
But you wanted me to keep going.

I should've stayed where I was
But the currents said "No
You must keep swimming."

I would've gone back for you, but
You said "Go, live."

If I'd only gone back for you,
Maybe things would've been totally different.

And no matter how many
Times I tried to drown and smoke you out
Of my head, regret always reminded me of failure.

And I will always fail
When it comes to the ghost of you...

I could've gone back for you
But you wanted me to keep going.

I should've stayed where I was...

Kissing Through a Ghost

I tune out profanity, it's simple.
I figured out how to stay frosty
Enough to make it through,
One day at a time.

'Cause it's incredible
How fast creatures
Will tear each other to pieces
If they think they smell weakness.

Their words escape their mouths
Like death birds' one way ticket,
Sorry about the mess below.

I tune it out, it's simple.

Sacramento, 1988.

And so my answer is headphones
And the places I go
Are everywhere, but here.

Goodbye blue sickness,

This is an upgrade from
Before, when I
Was a shadow.

The faces I miss the most
Can no longer enlighten
For they've become that definition.

When all is said and done,
It's still just me kissing through a ghost...

Spectre

For many years, I was nothing
But a spectre.
I'd weave my words into
The minds of warriors to keep the fire
Inside of them fed.
The first time I died inside was when you left,
No warning.
The heavens opened,
Like "Come on in."
I mourned you for years,
But I'm moving on now, no longer
Thinking about calling it quits.
I used to be a spectre,
And maybe that title still fits.
But I'm no longer hollow;
I'm no longer its vessel of sadness.

Worry

I worry about the future daily,
When hope is silenced
Like an assassination.
How will we ever grow into our
Best versions living like this?
So lost in our own imaginations.
Like travelling in the woods in the dark,
Trying to find our way back home
And never getting there.

I Can't Help but Think of You

It's the last of August:
I'm feeding the fire memories
While I watch flames dance around, as if
Alive with mind, body, and soul,
Chaotically turning things to ashes.
You were once a tree, and now
You're only fuel for
This faceless creature
That will expire just like the seasons do.
I'm getting ready to survive
Another Saskatchewan winter, it's true;
I'm praying for mild weather,
From November till March, all the way through.
I'm fuelled by my undying desire
To paint the city blue with language;
I am more than shades of Mars.
They said, "He's living on a far-off planet
All by himself, living in the aftermath of her absence.
He won't come back to full health.
He's long gone, lost cause.
No bright future or potential."
I proved them wrong twice,
When I severed the strings
Of delusion, and returned to my name

And the history of my existence.
I was born on the coldest night of '85,
And that's why January never leaves me completely.
It lives inside, and I thought it would get bored
Of haunting my eventless life.
No, I've only relapsed from my habit,
Of thinking of you on my birthday.
It's impossible not to,
And it absolutely guts me
Every single time without fail.

Chalk Line Everything

From the arms of one ghost to another,
Just my kinda luck,
Just my kinda love,
Left broken.

Chalk line everything,
'Cause this heart is pretty
Much a crime scene now,
Because of you.

And if you're
Still here when
I get back,
I'll know exactly
What to do next.

Torn

I really thought I'd found love once,
But she checked out early.
I never had you to myself,
I never had your heart.
Even with everything you had in the cards,
You gave it your all, you didn't hold back, dear star.
You were dealt a bad hand, you went far.
Even with everything wrong, you loved
God, like no one else, and I'm still torn that
He called you home so soon.
'Cause you were always a life-saving angel to me....

I Wanna Wish You Away

This isn't right, this isn't me.
And I don't wanna be so hostile.
I don't wanna feel so angry.
I don't wanna see betrayal,
And hearts barely breathing baby, like yours.
I wanna wish you away.

The Weight

No matter the day,
I still carry the weight
Of losing you.

Phantom Pain

Out of tar-covered night,
I thought I'd found an angel
To set my soul on fire, dead wrong.
Out of a dying blue mood I thought I'd fixed
What was damaged and gone.
I take back those sentences uttered
During inebriation.
Out in the city, I found keys
To locked doors,
Placed my demons in their cages
And sealed them in a vault underground to starve.
Out of compassionless January,
I thought that maybe her memory
Would stay buried,
But every year I drift
Back to her, and it absolutely
Crucifies my heart to the wall.

Pieces

Pieces of you remain,
Despite the gravestone.
I wonder if you ever check up
On me, because you were
The highlight of my life once,
And now you're January's ghost.
Please wait for me in the ever,
Or let me know I can move on,
Or let me go, release your hold
So I can sing a new song where
I won't break down in the chorus
Every night I'm alone.

Unable to Commit

Looking back at photos of my youth,
This picture stands out from the rest.
We're both young and smiling city wide,
But you were only a passing butterfly.
You'd float from one flower of attention
To the next, unable to commit to anything
More than friendship.
What an ancient wound.

Stitching Up the Wounds

My heart screams for release;
It's stitching up the wounds,
Sitting at a table of disorder,
But it's always golden aces.
My heart has gone through
Too much pain, and yet it's a survivor.
My heart's in deep psychosis,
Desperate to return to being stable.
My heart's after a quiet place
Where I can write in passerby
Seconds, and watch nature.
My heart's in sync with divine design.
At any second you could collapse if you
Live with your head down, and under a rock,
Stay humble in your conquest.
My heart grabs the mic and thunders,
"I am a warrior inside this shell!
Where are you, my love,
In all this smoke and shadow?"

If Only to Lose You

I dreamt of you again;
Like a bullet to the heart,
You left your mark on my life.
I wanted you to be mine, but time said no.
So off I go on my own,
To fill that hole in my chest that
Appeared after you left this world.
But I know I'll see you again,
My beautiful friend.
For why would we meet if only
To be separated by death?
If only to lose you...

For the Best

They say all things must end
And our love must die tonight.
So cut me off from you.
Don't answer the phone
Even If I call, okay?
It won't work,
And there's no need
To reopen our wounds
Or cause new ones.
It might be the worst,
But it's for the best.

This Isn't a Love Poem Is It?

My beasts, they watch over my shoulders
As I fall in lust once again.
Oh, darling starlight,
Do not forget me tonight;
I need to hold you tightly,
Surely more than you need me.
But do not turn me away
Without a chance to prove I'm worth the wait.
Oh, my endless ocean of mistakes,
They move like venomous snakes
In the tall grass.
When will I join
The icy winds of the north?
When will I be faint and disappear?

Wishing the Distance Wasn't So Far

Just so you know,
I won't be able to sleep tonight.
My mind will be picturing you
On your flight to Phoenix.
Take care of it; I put my heart in your pocket.
And as you fly away to witness a brand new city,
I will stay up counting stars in this one,
Wishing the distance didn't feel like acid rain,
And that I wasn't such a fool for the impossible.

Heat Bag

I hate this phone so much sometimes.
Sometimes I whisper to it…

"I really wish you were a different phone.
You're nowhere near as reliable as my flip phone,
With the keyboard.
I really loved that phone….

Not like you,
You heat bag."

The Long Goodbye

Tomorrow will be a heavyweight
Grudge match, because it will take
All your strength just to say it.
It hurts and it will
For quite some time, yes.
The long goodbye is painful,
Because the heart screams why!?

This Year Is an Avalanche

I carved hearts into diamonds,
Split a mountain with explosions,
Let her into my circle of friends,
But now it's broken like a grandfather clock,
Desperate to tick again.
This year is an avalanche,
And I may not be able to bounce back
And dig myself out alive.
Regardless of how hard I try to branch out,
The ruins around me are haunting,
Like the mummified remains
Of one thousand years of history.

Close I Cannot Do

I don't get too close to her;
She is pure flame,
And burning is something
She does a lot of these days.
See I won't get caught in her gaze,
I don't get too close to her
Because she has no name.
At least one that I care to know.

That Much Has Changed

I stay far away from smoke and mirrors.
I left my clouds behind and now I can actually
Look at my reflection and whisper,
"I love you, weathered soldier."
Those were words I never thought
I'd be able to say and mean.
That much has changed,
And I don't think I'll ever go back
To days of "I hate myself with a passion" again,
When I'm so close to the stars,
As if I could look up and see God gazing back into mine.

The Moment I Said Yes

She said, "Follow the neon blue painted trees
To find your way through the snowy forest."
I forget about God too often
And it causes me to sin
When I'm desperately trying to live honestly.
I'm really struggling to hold myself
Together in a pure fashion.
Pray for me to overcome
And I will close this chapter in time
With nothing to look back on besides
My old self who died
The moment I said yes to you.

Straight Edge

From the shadows and corners of the room,
I used to blend into negative spaces.
I used to be invisible even in the daylight.
I went from saying nothing,
To using my voice. The journey
Has been a rollercoaster of lessons,
Where I searched for my own crown.
I dared to want royalty in the quality of my words,
To find out what they're worth.
Maybe I'm too straight edge for you after all.

I'll Leave It in Your Hands

I used to think nothing could
Ever shake our world,
But there's a ton on the line.
My future is uncertain and
I don't know what'll become of this anthology.
I'll leave it all in your hands, Lord.
He said, "That's the safest
Thought you could ever have."

In You I Confide

I came to you to talk about brokenness. You said,
"I wish I could say
Recovery will move like a
Bullet train, but I can't win with them.
In you I confide,
You helped fixed my battle-scarred mind,
So don't forget who made mankind,
Don't forget who saved
You when you were a mess on the battlefield dying.
Don't sleep on your pile of money
And think you're going to Heaven,
Like maybe if I bribe Jesus I can get in?
It's better to know him now,
Than meet him at the end
When it's too late to be friends."

Sovereign

Take your weakness,
Run it over, staple it to the wall.
You saved me
From life's tornado.
It was you,
Making yourself known.
I did not, could not believe
So easily, but I found
My way to you.
And now I know,
You are unquestionably sovereign.
And I am only one of your paintings.

Whirlwind

Caught up in a whirlwind
Of snow and flame, your bitter island, I lost my way.
So, thank you for keeping me pure today, just nothing else,
You and you alone to hold my heart in your hand.
I'm not a villain like the ghosts before.
Just you and you alone to part the seas.

Do You Hear That Gentle Wind?

There's a voice, deep within yourself;
You can hear it when it's cemetery quiet,
When you stop talking and just listen.
Listen, do you hear that gentle wind?
God is trying to tell you He loves you,
But you're so consumed with instant
Gratification, like click, click,
Is it love or maybe not?
Nothing is above Him,
And you've sunk so low
Believing you're the exception
For you cannot hear
That gentle wind,
That gentle wind is a raft,
And you're drowning.

Candlelight Prayer

I can't help but come back to you;
You bring resolve to the pain I keep dead centre.
I get lost without your direction,
And I keep coming back to you,
Like I gotta breathe.
You fill me with hope
And candlelight prayer.
And I really can't help
But come back to you,
So you can repair my damaged battery.

Warmth (Part 2)

My heart is singing "Would you,
Could you, should you love me?
I would answer right back like gunfire.
I don't expect you to answer tonight,
For you are living in your mini world
And I'm a castaway in mine.
So far from a place to call home,
But longing to start a new one with you.
If you only knew my truth,
We could share the warmth
Until it leaves my hands."

Till We Grew Old

I keep coming back
To these memories of
The past when I would laugh
And thought these friends would
Age with me like mountains.
You left me behind in a trail of smoke.
We were supposed to keep
Fires going till we grew old.

I Hope You Sign Off, Without Suffering

Armed with pen, paper and open mind,
I search to find a better way to live.
And if you find it, hold on my friend.
I hope you enjoy yourself,
And leave this world in your sleep
Smiling from a good dream.

Sky City

"I hope the space between us doesn't destroy you."
That was the last thing she said to me.
She took a plane to the sky city.
And that was the last place she went.

But Baby, There Isn't Even a Way

With everything going on around me lately,
I've hardly had a chance
To make sense of this ongoing movie.
Poetry slinger off the clock,
Trying to hold myself together
And endure this apocalyptic weather.
And whether it's with you
Or without you I'm pressing on.
Can't stop the momentum now, don't want to.
With everything passing me by,
I just wanted you to stay and fix me.
But baby, there isn't even a way....

Author's Note

I want to thank Jesus Christ,
Mom, Dad, Annie, Dane, Oma, Shelly, Kent, Tyler,
Jessica, Tellwell, and you the reader
For picking up this book.

Printed in the USA
CPSIA information can be obtained
at www.ICGtesting.com
JSHW010241280723
45536JS00004B/10